AMERICAN MODERN HOME

Simon Jacobsen
Introduction by Paul Goldberger

Jacobsen Architecture + Interiors

AMERICAN MODERN HOME

RIZZOLI
NEW YORK

New York · Paris · London · Milan

*First published in the
United States of America in 2022 by
Rizzoli International Publications, Inc.
300 Park Avenue South, New York, NY 10010
www.rizzoliusa.com*

Photography is credited on page 224.

*Publisher: Charles Miers
Editor: Douglas Curran
Production Manager: Colin Hough Trapp
Managing Editor: Lynn Scrabis*

Designed by Beatriz Cifuentes

Printed and bound in China

2022 2023 2024 2025 2026 / 10 9 8 7 6 5 4 3 2 1

*ISBN-13: 978-0-8478-7205-3
Library of Congress Control Number: 2022932659*

*Visit us online:
Facebook.com/RizzoliNewYork
Twitter: @Rizzoli_Books
Instagram.com/RizzoliBooks
Pinterest.com/RizzoliBooks
Youtube.com/user/RizzoliNY
Issuu.com/Rizzoli*

Contents

THE GREAT MAN

Simon Jacobsen

"Not a shred of evidence exists in favor of the argument that life is serious, though it is often hard and even terrible. And saying that, I am prompted to add what follows out of it: that since everything ends badly for us, in the inescapable catastrophe of death, it seems obvious that the first rule of life is to have a good time; and that the second rule of life is to hurt as few people as possible in the course of doing so. There is no third rule."

—Brendan Gill

I don't know of many people who came through this world quite the way my father did. Looking back now at the truly fascinating personality and life of Hugh Newell Jacobsen with the eyes of a son who happened also to have been his business partner, I can claim a unique perspective on the man and an appreciation for those things that mattered to him.

"Fame is a gross distortion of a human being," wrote the author David Michaelis in an article for *Vanity Fair*, in reference to John F. Kennedy. Michaelis (a friend and one of our clients) might equally apply this sentiment to my father, meaning here, though, that there was a lot more to Hugh's personality than his public persona and buildings. Architects are very background people. They are often portrayed as quiet practitioners who spend their time "arranging the trilogy of the WC, kitchen and bedroom." This may be true for many, but it was not true of Hugh. Although he did those things and plenty, his personality, wisdom, and personal and professional styles made him a much larger person than his work and reputation alone might have allowed for. This caused people who had the experience to meet him to be somewhat in awe of the presence they encountered. Almost always attired in Pierre Cardin suits and Gucci this and that, he was rarely without a tie (and if he was, it is because he was on my sloop). At one of his many popular lectures or speaking engagements he would, like an actor about to step onstage, go into an alter ego of performance, and would stay that way until dinner and wine, later in the evening. With the trained eye, you could see him gradually deflate and return to earth before dessert. Beneath it all was humor and a kind of generosity of spirit that balanced and complemented the whole.

If one had to point to two early influential factors that went into the formation of the Great Man, as many in the firm called him, one would have to be that he had extreme learning challenges as a youth; and the other would be that he had been accepted and went to Yale, even though he had flat-line grades and no extracurricular experience other than beer. Being the man who he was, he publicly credited his father for pulling strings to get him there to anyone who would listen. It was, after all, the one part of Hugh Jacobsen he wanted everyone to know; he'd always had help. This created a kind of flip side of his personality where for much of his life he enjoyed being the radical modern architect who occasionally embraced a Brutalist aesthetics and very much saw himself on the outside and always looking in.

His career ascended in the early 1970s in Georgetown, a neighborhood in Washington, D. C., where he would live for almost sixty-five years. He made his start by designing kitchens, bathrooms, closets, and additions, until the Kennedy Democrats started moving to Georgetown. Here, his clientele became more well-heeled and known, which led him to such personal institutions as Paul and Bunny Mellon, Pamela Harriman, and, shortly after that, Jacqueline Kennedy Onassis, to name only a few. Here, my young parents, attractive and both considered "Yalies," were now part of the new smart social set of Washington, dining vith Katharine Graham, Ethel Kennedy, Ben Bradley, Shrivers of all kinds, and oceans of vriters and journalists. It would be another thirty ears before Hollywood would discover Hugh.

By 1977, the man was beginning to smell like et fuel and would spend fifty percent of his time way from home while working all over the ountry and in Europe. Work was so plentiful hat he was designing new commissions on irline airsickness bags, and, on landing, e would distribute them to staff architects, ometimes eight or ten different projects at once. Ie had three children, two were older and one vas younger by eight years to the eldest; that oung dyslexic lad was me. When looking at the nath, one doesn't get the vibration that I was a lanned bundle of joy. Because of the age gaps, was, in essence, an only child. This changed verything for my parents. My father would egin to take me everywhere: job sites, lectures, ravels. And the only place I could work would e his office.

After Yale in the late 1950s, Hugh was an NCO n the U. S. Air Force and was driving on a rainy ight with my mother on the then two-lane New Jersey Turnpike, near Edison, where they vere involved in a deadly head-on collision. Hugh's Austen-Healy hydroplaned and entered he oncoming lane, striking a truck and the ollowing car, a station wagon with a family in it areened under the now jackknifed truck, illing the driver. Hugh was hospitalized for ight months with a severe head injury. My nother survived miraculously unscathed, but ever spoke about the accident again. This frontal-lobe head injury would play a major role in Hugh's later years, culminating in early-onset dementia, in 2008. In my unscientific opinion, this terrible accident, along with inevitable guilt and anguish, may have unleashed his incredible creativity, as well, though at a terrible cost.

My father and I were not best friends, as so many people like to say of their close relationships of their parents, but we were so involved in the care of my mother and our work together that we became a kind of odd inseparable unit, one rarely seen without the other. At events, Hugh would often introduce me as "my partner, Simon," and I would quickly reply: "… as in business partner." Quite a few times we were misunderstood, and then later invited to after-parties where this misunderstanding became the gold standard in fast explanations and sudden polite exits.

In 2009, Hugh was waking up to the realization that I was beginning to build my own practice by simple virtue of association with him and the architectural playbook that was in my DNA. I was the younger, cheaper Jacobsen, and this caused the Great Man to reassess his position as well. It unfolded at a favorite restaurant of ours called The Prime Rib, in Washington, while listening to Dan Ruskin, our favorite piano standards virtuoso, at a table so close that it too could be considered part of the musical arrangement, where he stated that we should become partners indeed. The fact that he was willing, by his own design, to abandon the company he had spent fifty years building, to start a new one with me, still gives me pause. To my surprise, within a week, the legal documents were drawn up, the company's legal entity was moved to a state that had a more favorable partnership arrangements, and the new name established. Together we would be Jacobsen Architecture, LLC. After signing, notarizing this and that, and nervous glances there and forth, we were back at The Prime Rib, celebrating with my wife, Ruth, and my mother, and Dan Ruskin had converted a Cole Porter song "You're the Top" to include the rousing chorus "…You are all Jacobsen Architecture now!"

By age seventy-five, Hugh was no longer the architect who drove himself about in elegant British racing-green Jaguars, feeding the parking meter at abrupt awkward intervals. He traveled in a style that might lead one to mistake him for a high-powered federal prosecutor. Black town cars or large SUVs took him about Washington and different cities. When we traveled with staff architects, there were often several of these moving together; of course, as ever, a "proper lunch" was always one of the stops.

As the new century rolled in, Hugh was not really coming to terms with his changing world and the profession of architecture itself. In his 1960s orbit, the newsroom of the *Washington Post* looked identical to the drafting room of the Chicago office of Skidmore, Owings & Merrill. Long desks in a row, men in white shirts and ties bent over the boards, drawing or on the phone; the spaces were interchangeable. By 2001, the drafting room was now called a studio and it looked like mission control; computers were everywhere, cubicles, offices, it was all changing, and he hated it. But being no fool, he knew he had to move with the times or be blown away in the breeze like many of his colleagues who didn't.

The irony of this was that Hugh's personal heroes and close peers were all technically advanced practitioners who were on the forefront of building technology and methods, and Hugh himself was a huge risk-taker in stretching the longevity and physics of practical materials to achieve what he had designed. He explained this to his clients with a slight Etonian clip: "It is not a Chevy but a Bentley, and the endeavor requires a little more attention…."

Our partnership created a subtle realignment and shift in the volumetric arrangement of pavilions and interiors in our work. The detailing of exterior forms became more aggressive and sparse in consequence of new materials and the methods they require. This allowed us to clean up the purity of the lines, including gutter- and downspout-less roof forms such as at Bird House and Harbor Hill (shown on pages 14 and 144, respectively). The photos here will also show a conscious effort to take on clients who are, one might say, not so much "captains of industry" and to embrace those with wide-ranging in interests and tastes—ultimately designing houses for families that have been more adaptable, and, one might go on to say, "less Bentley and more Cadillac." This is something we learned in 1998 when we designed the LIFE Magazine Dream House.

Over the past twenty years, prospective clients who inquired about our work would often state that we were mostly out of touch with a larger contingency of people because our work was too large or too remote. We have striven to change this perception and the associated reality. However, the objective of always chasing after ever more finely rendered detail and the refinement of American iconic building forms remains a primary force driving the firm forward, and with a new direction that you will see. Interior rooms are more exclusive of one another and have their own pavilions rather than shared spaces. The challenge of hiding light sources and subtlly revealing space continues with its own urgency. The poetry of voids and planes and how they interact with people who pass through them has always defined our design ethos, but even more so now. Where this quality was once just another feature, it is now the whole point.

The Great Man died on March 4, 2021.
With his spirit as a guiding light, the firm carries on into a new century and toward a brave new world of space and light.

INTRODUCTION

Paul Goldberger

Hugh Newell Jacobsen never had any patience for the tiresome debates about modern versus traditional architecture, and neither, I suspect, does his son and partner, Simon. Hugh Jacobsen did not take one side or the other in that dispute; he transcended it, making an architecture that was very much his own, and which always made you wonder why anyone ever thought that modern and traditional were considered opposite ways of designing buildings. Jacobsen's work was, in one sense, as crisply modern as a house, or an apartment, could be. It was always sharp and often white, with a light, tensile quality to it, and consistently urbane, even when it was not urban. Jacobsen had a modernist sensibility like none other, crafted very much out of the elements of traditional architecture—gables most of all, but also porticos and pergolas and windows and dormers and fireplaces and nooks and crannies. He saw the pure geometric shapes that were often hidden within the architectural forms of the past, and he distilled them down to a pure essence, making them simple rather than ornate. And then he put them together into a composition that was one part abstract, minimalist sculpture, and one part celebration of the symbolic meaning of the traditional house.

His death in 2021 at 91 was a loss for architecture on many levels: he was as refined as he was creative, and passionate and knowledgeable about the whole world of architecture, far beyond what was on his own drawing board. And he was unusual among leading architects in that he was happy to focus his practice on residential design, seeing it not as a time-consuming occupation to be borne until bigger institutional and commercial commissions came his way, but as the best thing an architect could do. In fact, the firm had plenty of larger commissions as well, but domestic architecture was where it always seemed that Jacobsen's heart lay. Where else, after all, did you connect so closely with people than in giving shape to their houses? He had a fascination for the way in which different lives could inspire an architect to make different houses that were nevertheless part of a coherent oeuvre. It is not a surprise that he became a friend to so many of his clients.

Hugh Jacobsen was different from many of his architectural colleagues in another way, too, which is that he planned logically for the next generation of his practice. He was fortunate to have had an architect son who took pleasure in sharing his practice and, more importantly, shares the philosophical approach that underlies it. Simon joined his father in 1994, and the firm name was changed to Jacobsen Architecture in 2009 to reflect the fact that for more than a quarter of a century most of their work has been a joint effort. Almost all the work in this book was directed by Simon Jacobsen, whose own commentary on each project serves as the text, making it clear that while he has built on the direction set by his father, he has continually adapted it to new places, new programs and new clients.

A case in point is the sprawling estate known as Harbor Hill, overlooking the harbor in the island of Nantucket. Here, strict local building regulations, which were created to encourage traditional architecture and prevent overt expressions of sculptural modernism, require that all houses have peaked roofs and gray shingles and discourage the construction of large villas. The peaked roof is a Jacobsen trademark, but the other requirements were not as easy to meet. Hugh Jacobsen helped to conceive an ingenious plan that divided a twenty-two-thousand-square-foot house into what is, in effect, a village of small, contiguous pavilions, composed elegantly around an arrival court, an open lawn, a pool area and the view across the water to the town of Nantucket. The structures are all shingled, and their soft, gray textured facades work as well with Jacobsen's concept of abstracting the traditional house as the firm's more characteristic white horizontal clapboard. The meticulously arranged composition breaks up the scale of the house when viewed from the water and hides the size of the structure from the entry drive, where the pavilions reveal themselves in a gradual processional sequence.

Different as the Nantucket house is from many other Jacobsen projects, it shares with most of the others a quality of expansiveness masked in a certain modesty. It is a characteristic of Jacobsen houses that the spaces within them feel generous and they are rarely cramped; the rooms flow, and as often as not they are stretched out to allow circulation space to be a significant element of the architectural experience. Yet they are never grandiose or bombastic, and there is a feeling of intimacy to every Jacobsen project, no matter how large.

Intimacy, precision, lightness, and a fondness for symmetry where it doesn't get in the way of common sense—these are qualities that marked Hugh Jacobsen's work early on, and which Simon Jacobsen has maintained and extended in new directions. Of course, some of the firm's trademarks have not changed: the gridded bookshelves of thin, light verticals and horizontals, for example, or the fondness for classic modern furniture pieces like Le Corbusier's Petit Confort chairs or Mies van der Rohe's Barcelona chair, often done in a striking white upholstery, which makes them feel both old and new. Like the white walls that seem to be universal, the bookshelves of grids and the reliance on classic modernist furnishings are present not just in the firm's freestanding houses, but in apartment renovations and other interior projects. They are constants that have not varied on Simon Jacobsen's watch.

When you look at a project like Bray House in Kittery Point, Maine, where a seventeenth-century balloon-frame house on the waterfront was restored and made the centerpiece of a new Jacobsen composition, it becomes clear both how well the principles of the firm's design philosophy have held, and how much they can stretch to encompass new situations. In this case the key compositional idea was to take advantage of the fact that the old house was set parallel to the waterfront, which led Simon Jacobsen to array several small cottage-like units perpendicular to it, giving the old house pride of place as the only portion of the complex with its long side facing the water. To give the seventeenth-century house further distinction, it is the only unit set apart, connected to adjacent wings by discreet glass links. The other cottage-like sections are not separate pavilions but masses joined together. The old house sets the tone for the entry facade of the whole structure, with windows cut out of a solid front, reflecting the reserved nature of colonial architecture. On the more private waterfront side, however, the new wings are sheathed mostly in glass, and only the seventeenth-century wing retains its solid facade and punched windows, further emphasizing its unique role as the dowager presiding over her youthful progeny. The message here is that the newer wings are allowed some freedom in private, so long as they behave in public. Jacobsen's underlying modernist instincts are never in doubt, but neither is the determination to tame these instincts into something discreet and proper. Seventeenth-century gentility, Jacobsen is telling us, still has its place, but it does not need to control everything that happens once you get past what the public is most likely to see.

This is, I think, another key aspect of the work of both Jacobsens: it is modernism with manners. There is always understatement in front, and a respect for privacy; exuberance is kept in check until after you cross the threshold. The love of the tiny cottage shape, almost like a Monopoly house, pervades everything, and gives a hint of playfulness to the public and the private sides of every one of these houses—but never so much as to suggest that playfulness is all the architect has in mind. Simon Jacobsen, like Hugh Jacobsen before him, believes most of all in making a modernism with delicacy and subtlety, a modern architecture that aspires to the elegance and civility of the ages.

TWELVE HOUSES

BIRD HOUSE

Napa, California

The last house Hugh was involved in was in Napa, California, just north of the town itself. Sitting high on a bluff overlooking its own vineyard and the valley, the two-thousand-square-foot house and pool is a perch for a retired advertising executive from San Francisco.

Being mindful of seasonal fires, the exterior of the house was constructed of fire-resistant materials, including a metal roof, porcelain-based clapboard siding, and PVC trims.

Immediately upon opening the front door, the view of the valley is revealed. The California sun casts long, elegant shadows through the sunscreens; the little dormer windows in the roof light the interior smartly from high above.

The floor is Navona travertine, the same stone from which Rome was built. A long hall, typical of the firm's work, connects the two bedrooms on either side of the house, the open living room, and the kitchen uniformly and intuitively. There is no base or crown molding per usual, just the expression of the simple volumetric forms and walls dancing to the rhythm of solid planes and voids.

The exterior excludes gutters and downspouts to emphasize the simple linearity and refinement of the building forms, reminiscent of days gone by. A study of early agricultural shapes and buildings of Napa led the archtiects to the staggered and shifting forms.

When seated in the living room, an infinity-edge pool and spa casts doubt that there is anything other than water and mountains between the two. The reflection of the hill on the water is marvelous.

A bit of the past makes itself known at the front door. A door detail first designed by Hugh in 1960 reemerges as the front door of Bird House. The Jacobsen family house had this style of front door, as well, when it was designed in 1968.

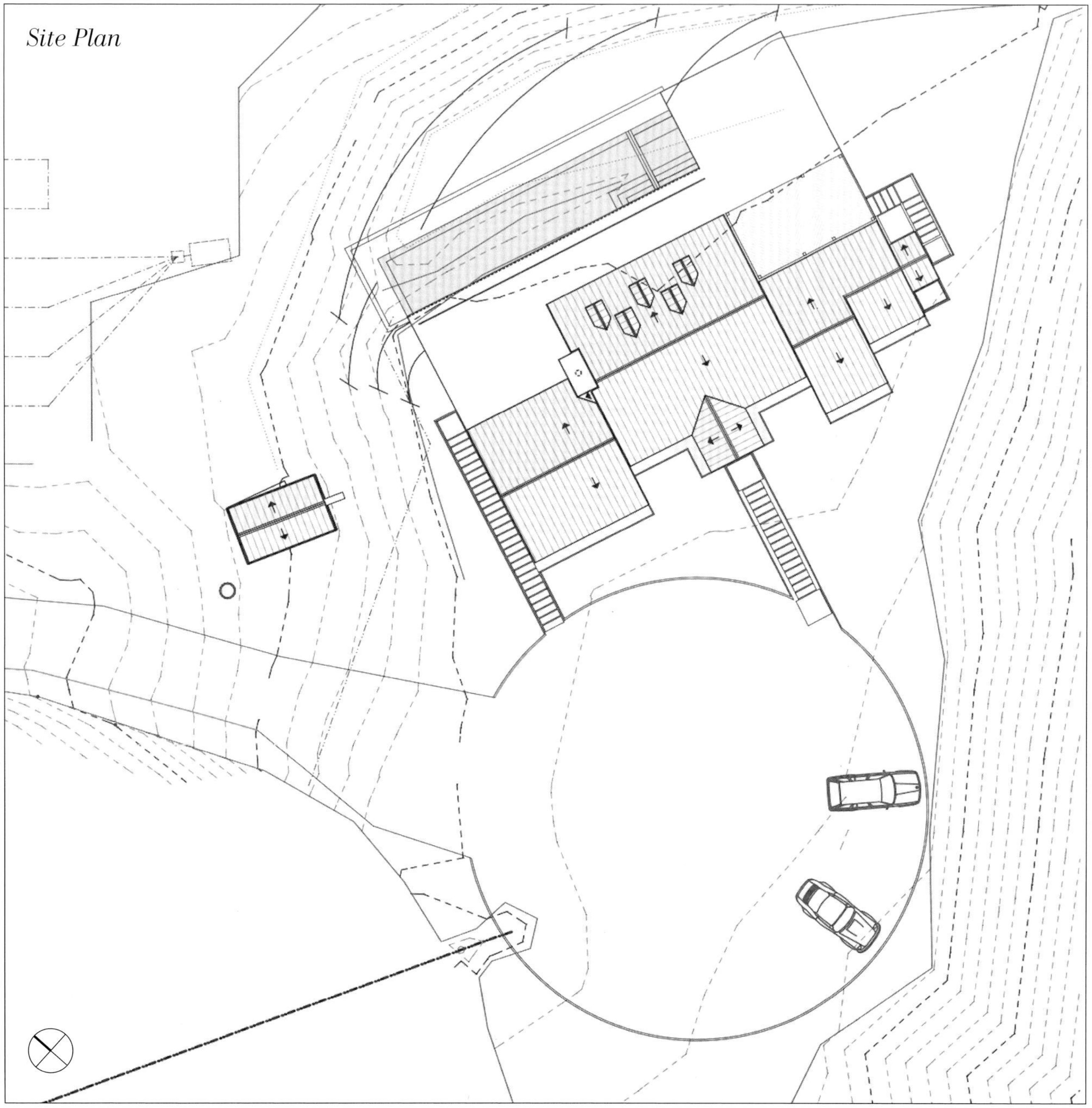
Site Plan

Section

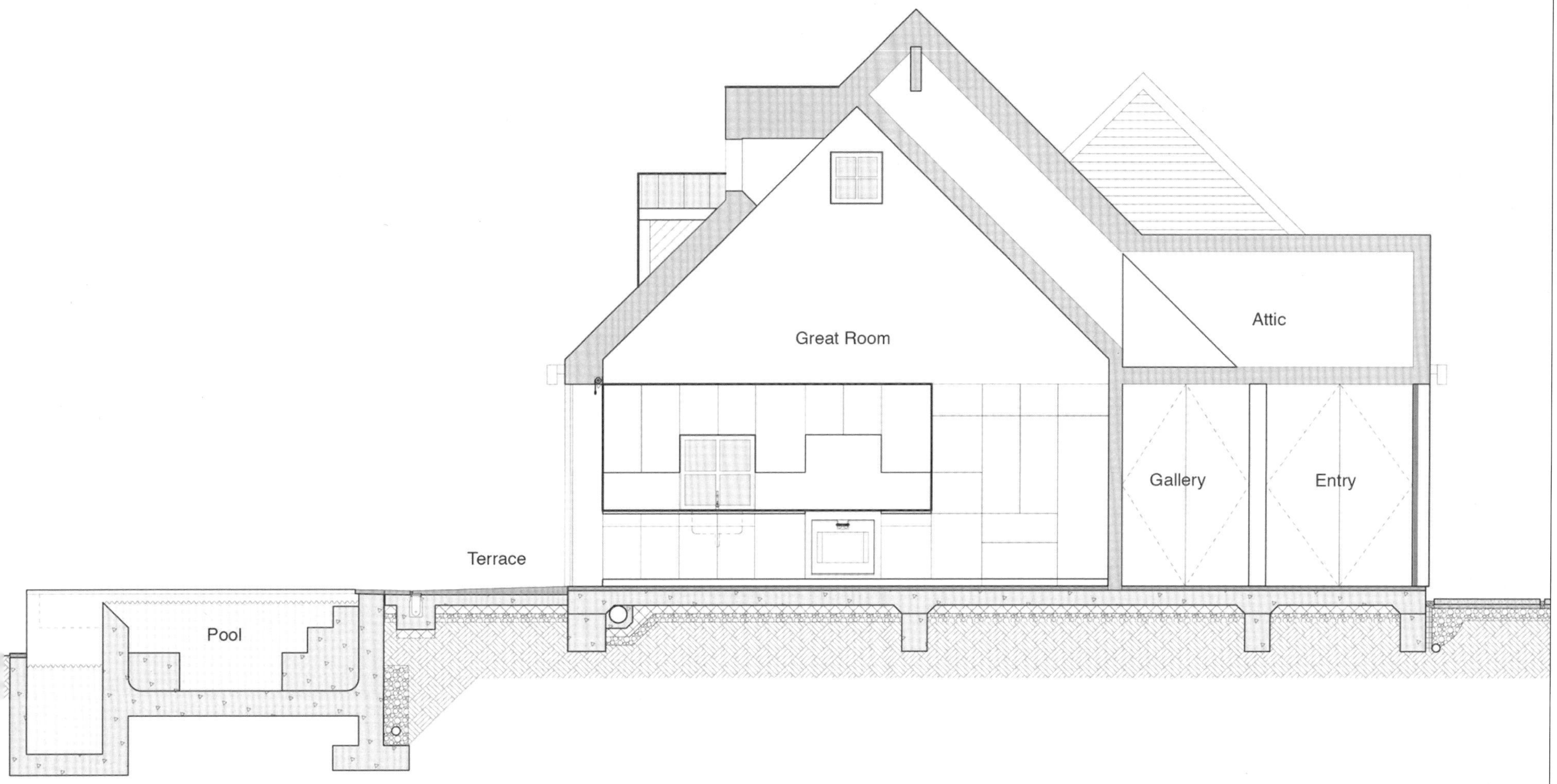

Next two spreads
In the effort to maximize the elegant geometry of this classic American agricultural form, all gutters and trim boards are removed to reveal the true essence of the structure's simplicity.

The autumn colors of Napa Valley's vineyards are accentuated by the infinity-pool edge as captured in this photo by Simon Jacobsen on final inspection.

The design of the pool and its bottom color were carefully studied so as to mimic the California sky at midday. The canvas of white and glass beside it causes the colors of the surroundings to pop.

he butt-joined, cornerless glass causes the roof visually float above the walls while at the me time defying gravity, all to emphasize the n, air, and delight.

'he namesake of the project was one of the last
lements to be designed. Here, a birdhouse
ontains the pool equipment and garden tools.

The Jacobsen sunscreen has gone through a long history of modifications and improvements. The primary purpose is not to shield people from rain but rather to diffuse the sunlight, which is constantly changing to cast shadows that play across terrace or table.

The kitchen allows for seating at an island that does not impose on guests the insistency of sitting on a stool, but rather allows use of a proper chair, as our Creator envisioned for us. Dramatic light and shadows are cast down on the counters in the mornings and evenings from the six small dormers above.

THE NEW ARCHITECTURE OF WINE
FROM THE LAND

The firm treats large spans of glass not as voids but as reflective planes that are lit from above. At night this leads the eye to blur the thresholds between indoor and outdoor, creating a harmonious merger between house and nature.

SMITH ROW

Georgetown, Washington, D. C.

In 1791, as Pierre Charles L'Enfant was laying out the city of Washington under the watchful eye of George Washington, an aesthetic problem began to emerge in the seat of the new republic, and was being reported by foreign newspapers by 1805. The new city had very well-designed federal buildings and spaces but had terrible roads and unsophisticated houses with little to no neighborhood planning. These problems contributed to the city's designation as a "hardship" post for diplomats until the 1920s.

A movement was undertaken, with eyes on the Adams White House, to demonstrate that Washington could be not only an exciting experiment but architecturally significant as well. Several "serious" residential buildings were started along Pennsylvania Avenue and were given the nod by the president. Other endeavors were launched in then gritty Georgetown, one of which was Cox Row and this—the crown jewel—at Smith Row.

Although a modern architect, Hugh Jacobsen had a career graced with some very serious historical renovations; examples range from Hôtel de Talleyrand in Paris to a portion of the U. S. Capitol. In the midst of these were dozens of detailed and complex restorations in Georgetown, Annapolis, West Virginia, Massachusetts, and many more, which earned high praise from restoration specialists and professional societies for accurate historical detailing and a larger canvas vision.

The house's previous owner for more than thirty years was Herman Wouk, the Pulitzer Prize–winning author of *The Caine Mutiny*, who lived here until the mid-1980s. On the mantel during our initial walk-through were Captain Queeg's stainless balls, a gift from Humphrey Bogart and inscribed: "To Herman, from Bogart." The house had a secret escape room, as members of Wouk's own family had been killed by the Nazis during World War II. In one room stood a rotating bookcase, behind which was a four-foot-by-four-foot room with a wooden stool, a princess phone on the wall, and spilled nine-millimeter rounds on the carpeted floor.

The house at Smith Row was not really a historical restoration but an intervention. Like many period urban houses in Georgetown and in English cities, the kitchen and main dining area were in the basement with unimpressive ceiling heights of six feet five inches. The firm's typical approach when going underground is to make the ceilings taller than those of the aboveground floors in order to reduce the "basement effect," but in this house, the living room ceiling is fourteen-feet high, making the usual approach impractical. So, the architects pulled out the two lower floors under the living room to reconfigure a new proper kitchen and dining room with nine-foot ceilings and a breakfast terrace.

The house also had some sufferings in its original design, one of which was rather small rear windows on the main floor as well as a root cellar and rumored slave quarters on the lower level in the rear and garden. With much ado and some steel, these would be removed to create a lower breakfast terrace and the living room would be rewarded for patiently waiting two hundred years for some sunlight. (The living room doors are

now new sliding pocket doors, also with a screen of matching mullions.) To prevent falling onto the terrace below, nearly invisible one-inch-thick glass railings stop such misadventures and awkward social departures.

The house is now complete with our signature Jacobsen eggcrate bookshelves, which are not only a system for books and magazines, but literally a color delivery system. By refining the structure down to three-eighths of an inch, the shelves themselves mostly melt away to reveal only the colorful spines of the volumes. A bit of visual trickery is of course involved: the shelves get smaller in their ascent to the ceiling, acting as an involuntary trompe-l'œil for the observer. To emphasize this, all light switches and door handles are also located at thirty inches above the floor.

Throughout the rest of the house are reconfigured bedrooms in the discipline of period homes such as this; closets, a private office, and all interior doors and openings were replaced with the firm's signature full-height doors. The pimary bedroom dressing room upstages much of the refined design of the second floor with a custom, multitiered shoe-shelving system that would surely catch the eye of Mrs. Marcos. The main living room wall, a five-story structural bearing wall, was inverted to accommodate the owner's art. The wood floors of the main floor and dining level are a rich stained walnut.

A black-bottom pool was added, and under that is an impressive array of geothermal loops that heat and cool the five-story masonry manse efficiently.

Cross Section

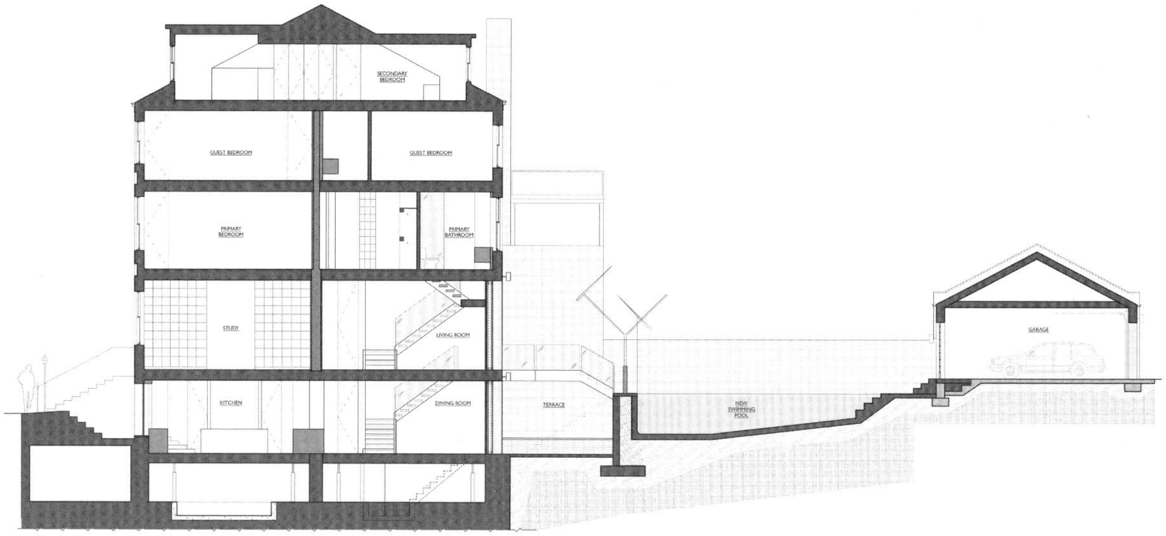

Floor Plans

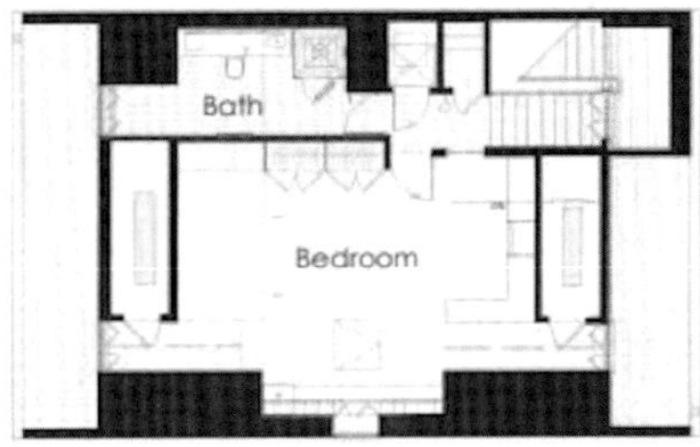

Fourth Level

Third Level

Second Level

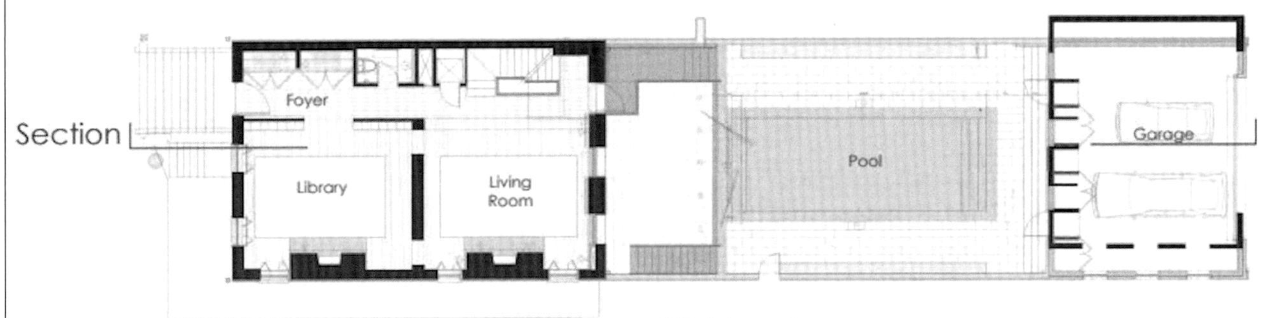

First Level

Lower Level

*'he black-bottom pool serves not as surface
) reflect the sky, but rather it acts to absorb
ght into a shimmering abyss.*

Many early East Coast urban houses have their kitchens in the basement, as is the case here. The kitchen can easily transform from casual family dining to formal catering by using movable walls (now hidden) that divide the two spaces.

VIKING

J.S. BACH
PLEYEL
PARIS

A purist fireplace, sans mantel, is complementary to the owner's refined midcentury furnishings and objects. The "kerf," a black reveal that separates the intersection of the wall and the ceiling, gives license to the space to float.

Bookcases and sliding shoe cases utilize the firm's renowned eggcrate system of shelving to house the owner's collections.

HONEYMOON COTTAGE

Kennett Square, Pennsylvania

When you drive through this area of southeastern Pennsylvania, Andrew Wyeth comes to mind. Not by coincidence, the owners are good friends with the Wyeth family, who would play a part in the little nine-hundred-square-foot cottage's design and site placement.

The owners visited the architects in the Georgetown office to discuss the design of a new guest cottage for their 1780s house. Their children were older now and the main house was getting small during holidays. They required a secondary dwelling that was "close, but just far enough."

In the rear of the old stone house was an orchard that had a vast field sloping up to a handsome apex. This is Wyeth country, of course, and, as Simon recalls, "I was struck that I may have been looking at a double of the hill in Wyeth's painting *Christina's World*. We found the placement and orientation of the house there, as if you yourself are Christina."

In many cases, when one is told "You will be staying in the cottage…," it can bring on a sense of dread and a personal questioning of just how much your hosts care for you; so the objective was to create something that was simple on the outside but transformative and exciting on the inside. The architects' favorite line to use with respect to this quality (and admittedly an irreverent one at that) is this: "Every house should have a Jesus Christ; you walk inside and you say, 'Jesus Christ!'"

Gone would be the fox-hunting paintings, red rooms, and brass chandeliers typical of the area, and instead would appear a sleek two-bedroom space that disrupts the notion forever of a small center-hall Colonial house. The recessed paneled front door is encased in a vestibule, so as to protect an entrant from the weather. It has an exterior chevron door that is white on the outside and red on the in. In the Quaker tradition, when the family has a daughter of marrying age, the father would paint the inside of the door red to indicate her availability. Given that this cottage was to be used by growing children, we thought this to be rather fitting.

Direct lighting is delivered in two ways, recessed spots and mini pendants that allow for the best light on a wall with a sloped ceiling. The floors are a rich, high-gloss porch paint for durability and light reflection, which also does nicely as a canvas for the owner's art.

White spaces reflect all spectrums of color, ergo "White is the presence of all color," as Hugh would say. Rooms that are painted yellow or red reflect only those colors.

A white room with furnishings, books, and art is a repeater of the space's reflective objects and artful attributes. This is why galleries are not painted black; they treat the room as a canvas that also serves copious amounts of wine and crackers.

A glass-railing ladder/stair intentionally blocks your view as you enter the front door; beyond that is a fireplace surrounded by ten-foot-by-nine-foot pieces of glass, with an open gable, as well. Left and right are the bedrooms and en suite bathrooms staggered on opposite sides of the living room. Hidden behind louvered doors are a kitchenette and laundry. The open-riser stair leads to a glass-enclosed loft that is ideal for young children and naps. The loft floor is a series of large Sunbrella cushions stuffed with goose down, of the kind one would perhaps find on a deck of a fine Hinckley yacht.

Site Plan

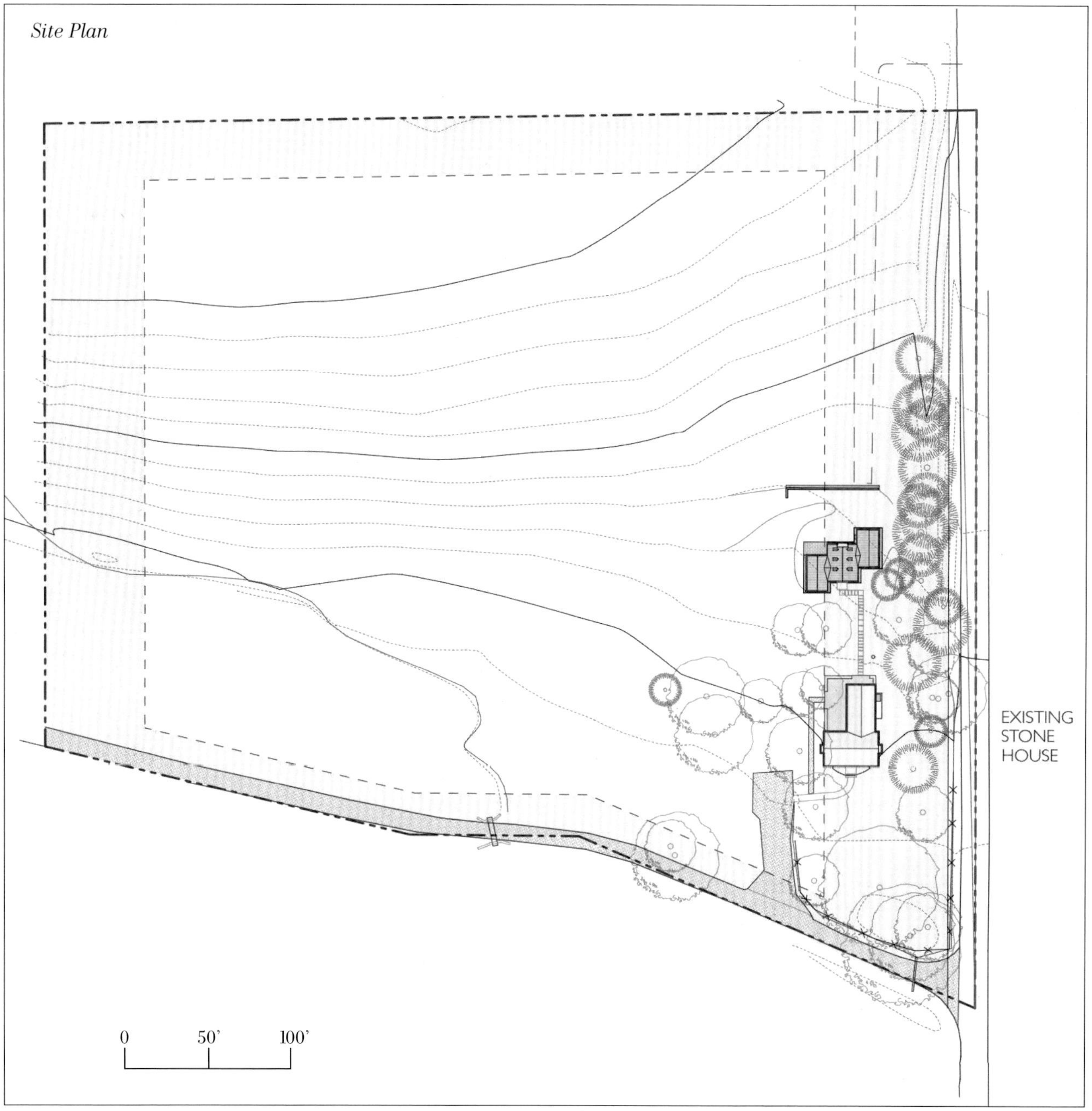

Site plan (above) shows relationship of previously existing stone house and, above it, the cottage. Cottage entry (opposite) with signature red outer doors.

Plan

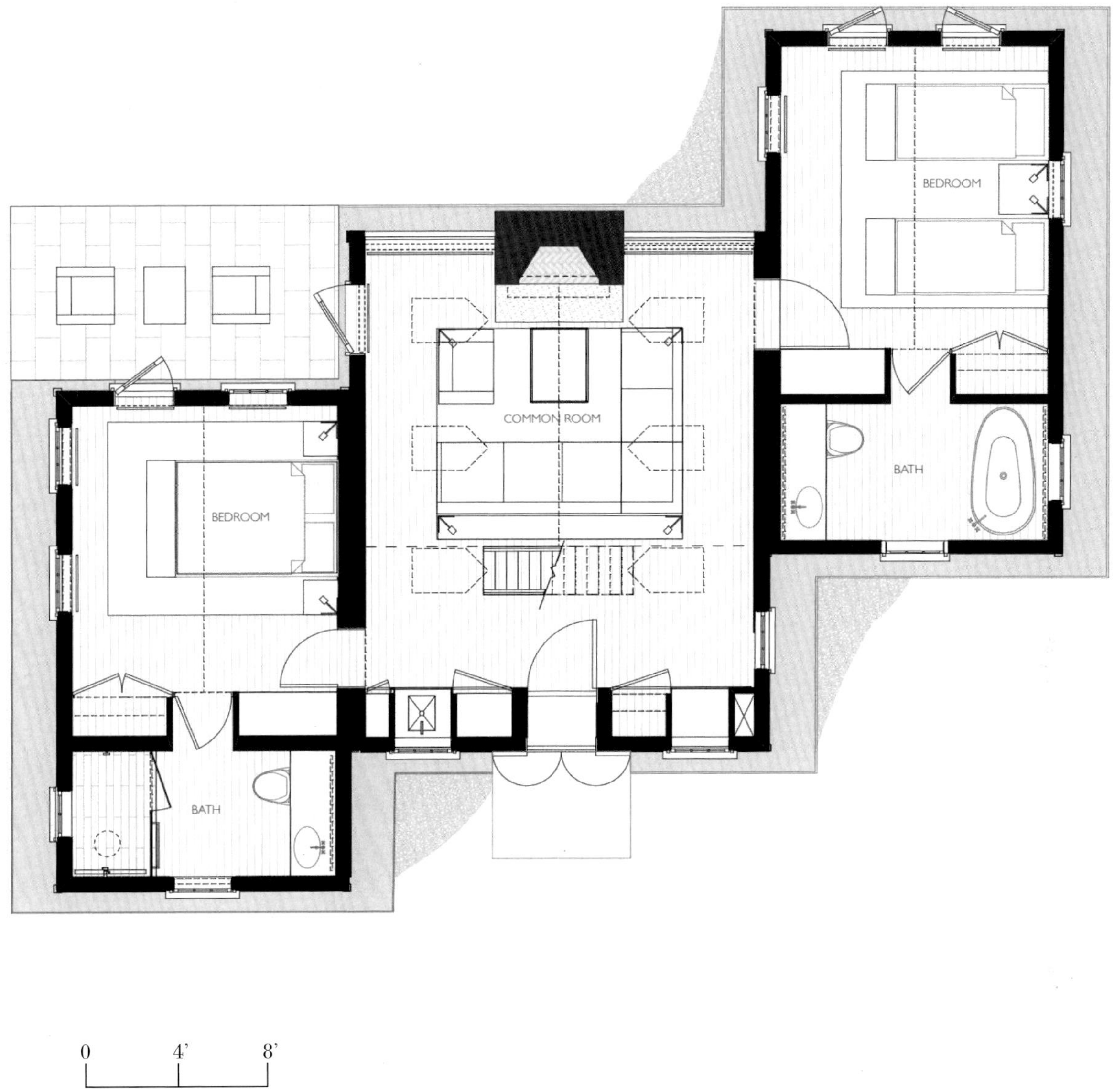

A staggered, offset floor plan softens the center mass of the pavilion so that it does not sit too proud or compete with the main house.

The grandchildren's sleeping loft (above) is adorned with goose down and pleated canvas floor cushions and framed by glass railings.

To answer the age-old question about the chicken and the egg: here, the egg tub came first, and the house was built around it in place, because of its size.

Nothing is more obvious in this photo than the saying "White is the presence of all color." The owner's post–Revolutionary era flag ignites the room against the cobalt evening sky of Southern Pennsylvania. A white Le Corbusier Grand Confort chair of goose down sits in tranquility with a Jacobsen X-table of stone and Lucite. The horse weather vane that is above the fireplace also hides a television, and the frame is automated to rise when engaged.

The cottage's placement and orientation was designed to invoke the view in Andrew Wyeth's painting Christina's World.

The manipulation of scale is apparent here on the cottage's rear elevation. The staggering of the pavilions and the reduction in size of the wood clapboard siding makes the nine-hundred-square-foot little, heroic manse seem even smaller than it really is. The success of secondary buildings is always in their relationship with the main house, which they must never ignore.

CHIC CONVENIENCE

Georgetown, Washington, D. C.

The small, fifteen-hundred-square-foot wood-framed house was originally built during the Civil War in 1863. Georgetown become a name and a social destination in the 1950s during the Eisenhower administration when the young incoming senators, journalists, artists, and thinkers started moving to the old neighborhood for its Federal architecture and refined wood-framed Greek Revival dwellings. Before that, Georgetown was a busy active seaport, and the seedy underbelly of active ports came with it.

Simon Jacobsen moved into the little two bedroom house after architecture school in 1994 in an effort to assist his father with his ailing mother. The care she required was affecting his practice and his health as well. Their house was across the street. Simon expected to be there only a few years, but the demand of his services to his father's firm and his ill mother kept him there for twenty-six more years.

A two-bedroom house was too small for Simon's new wife and children, and he needed to stay close as his father and mother were beginning to need more assistance, so when the identical house next door went on the market, they scooped it up with hope and skepticism for a successful joining of the two. The main issue was this: would the floor align once they took down the dividing party walls. To his surprise they did exactly, which led to the speculation, and then the fact, that the two little houses were actually built as one and divided before completion.

Once joined and the walls removed, the main entry space became one large room with only the existing three fireplaces and plumbing popping through. A central core was designed that would house two fireplaces, coat closets, bar, pipes, ducts, and, then in the elbow would be a library and study on the north side. Because the family had young children, a "circus" was created so they could ride their big wheels and other modes of toddler transport around in a large circle. This eventually evolved into running, then teenage apathy.

This would be the first house in many years where the architect painted all the floors white. Not just any white, but a super-high-gloss, always-looks-wet white exterior porch paint. At the same time, this would influence Hugh to paint a house in Nantucket, on Liberty Street, to undertake the same look for reasons of economy and "chic convenience." This translates in Jacobsen speak to *it may be the cheapest thing to do, but it is also best idea so far*. Several other houses would follow for the same reason that year.

But the house had to do more than exercise children—it had to entertain, too. A bar behind two doors that mimicked a wall hid the parents' vices, and could be closed off quickly in case the vicar came to visit. Large closets and storage were designed within the two-story core and would accommodate the immense clutter a young family accumulates with reptilian memory.

The house also had a lower-level catering kitchen with a long thirty-foot counte,r which is unusual for a Georgetown house. This oddity offered both family and visitor surprise and delight.

Garden Level

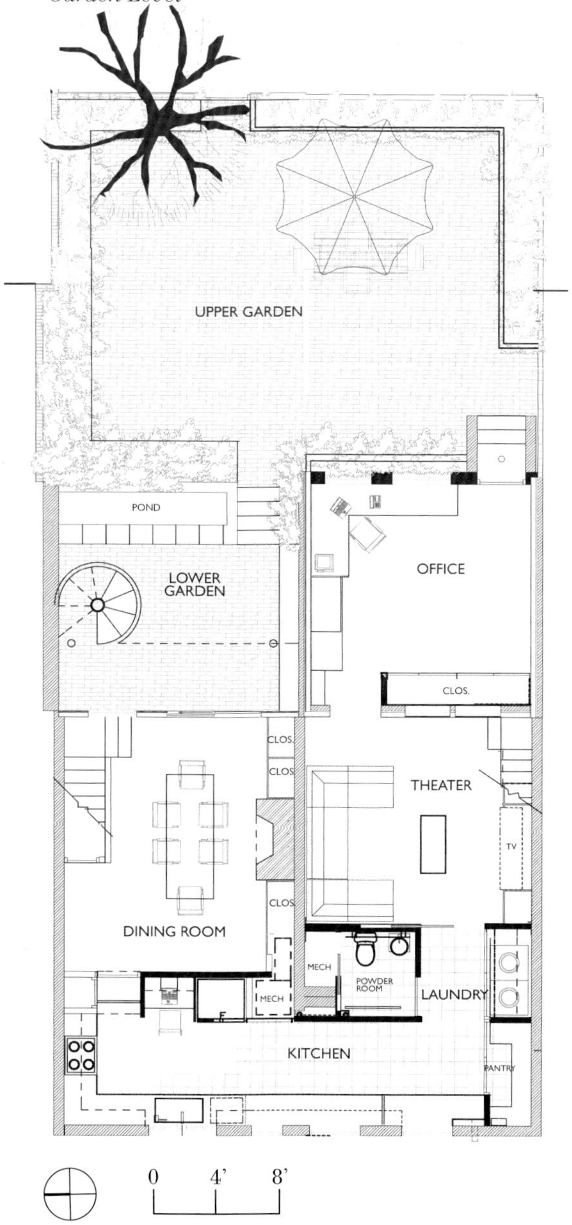

Main Level

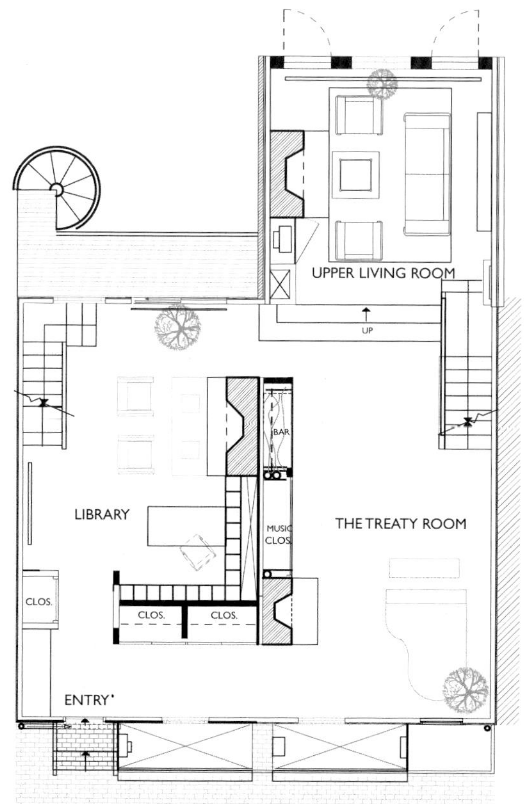

Upper Level

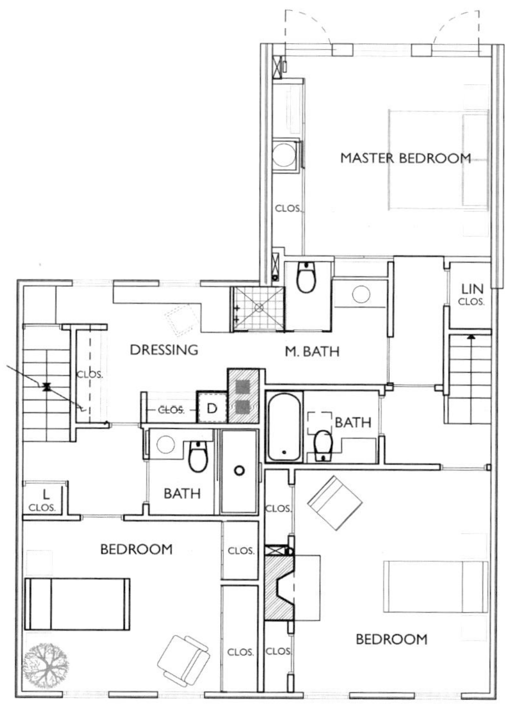

Joining two houses and getting them to work correctly can drive a person to drink. Here (above) we see the new central core that was created to provide plumbing and heating distribution throughout the three levels while unifying the fireplaces and compartmentalizing bookcases, bar, and closets.

1355

THE PHOTOBOOK
Wine

imon Jacobsen's desk is simply two planes antilevered off the bookcase. The glass table, lso by Jacobsen, acts as a reflective solid.

s the invisible walls part, a bar is revealed hat transforms the space from one thing to omething quite another.

CALVERT STREET APARTMENT

Washington, D. C.

The firm is always giddy when it gets a project in Washington, which eliminates the need to get on airplanes. This project was for a couple who directed the architects to pull out the stops and combine two apartments into one. Modernists down to their socks, the couple had admired the firm's work for decades and directed them with a very specific program for a single bedroom with spaces for dining and entertaining, an office, large bathroom, powder room, and a sleek kitchen. Once the existing elements were removed from the space, work set out to redesign the two spaces and create a strong central axis that would combine all the rooms uniformly.

The firm has long believed in what it calls *hello space* when one enters a house or apartment. This is achieved by providing at the entrance a slightly exaggerated, somewhat minimalist open area that allows one to take in the design and delight in the rooms immediately as your coat is being taken.

To gain control of the interaction, a full-height plane of frosted, low-iron glass was installed to shield the surprise of the awaiting living room just beyond. A piano and an array of Jacobsen-designed furniture is arranged in a comfortable seating group, from the firm's X-tables to sofas and floor lamps, for occasional reading and fond reminiscences of the architects.

A once-concealed bar facing the living room was reopened to reveal excitement and a youthful approach. The owners, fans of hosting occasional cocktail parties, wanted a gem of a bar to sparkle. The architects lined the "embibery" with glass shelves and low-iron mirror and glass to twinkle some reflective light back into the space like a Fifth Avenue Tiffany display window of watches.

From the living room, one looks through a set of frosted-glass pocket doors to the dining room, where there is an eggcrate bookcase that also serves a casual buffet if needed. The dining table, designed by the frim, is a single-leg configuration that is bolted directly to the concrete floor. This eliminates the collision of legs and knees and gives more flexibility to seating different arrangements of guests.

"To ruin the surprise would be cruel," said Simon Jacobsen to Hugh. As one enters the front door, the intentionally open "hello space" is divided in two by a seemingly nonsensical luminescent frosted plane.

Floor Plan
New Walls
Existing Walls
Terrace
Living
Dining
Laundry
Music
Bedroom
WC
Kitchen
Closets
Glass Wall
Office
Foyer
Stairs
Bath
Hall

ALBRECHT DÜRER

A sliding frosted-glass door allows for complete separation between living and dining areas when entertaining. Eggcrate bookshelves beyond help frame the space's offeringfs and trick the eye into imagining that the ceiling is higher than it really is.

THE HAMPTONS
BRITANNICA ATLAS

Jacobsen-designed Dominican *chairs and a bench in stainless steel accompany the first Jacobsen* X-tables. *Sliding artwork in a new invisible ceiling track hides the television. Inconspicuous light fixtures create a mysterious ambience.*

:ggcrate bookcases have a dual personality as hey can easily be modified to hold any number f objects; here, in the bedroom, the little cubes be-ome an array of a shoes-and-boots library.

BEACH HOUSE

Aquinnah, Massachusetts

One of the finest drives a person can take on Martha's Vineyard is when you travel east to west from Edgartown to Aquinnah and Gay Head. This is only matched by the long driveway of bleached white oyster shells as you complete your journey and enter Beach House.

At the end of the drive sit two small shingled pavilions with no adorning white trim boards or plank-frame windows typical of the zip code. To emphasize the simple shapes of the traditional cottages, the forty-five-degree white-cedar shingles have no gutters and downspouts to distract the eye. Or, as Hugh liked to say: "We do not put plumbing on the outside of our buildings."

The motivation behind this simple approach toward the first buildings is to suggest intimacy and to not betray the large scope of the conjoined six-thousand-square-foot whole. As you move toward Vineyard Sound and the front door, the house reveals itself slowly as falling down a gentle dune. The house is in fact two stories and four bedrooms.

The owners, who hail from Washington, D. C., are also owners of a house that Hugh did in Florida in the late 1980s, so they are very familiar with the canvas.

With owners who are avid readers, the house has two libraries; one as you enter and another in the lower half of the house. The entrance is unique for a beach cottage because as one closes the door, the visitor sees none of the expected nineteenth-century Vineyard references but is now in the first row of a serious modernist orchestral movement. A unique glass and marble credenza directed by the owner leads the way to a glass overlook that peers down below to a living room of glass-and-teak decks looking out to the sound. To get there is the real adventure, as you must walk across a ballistic-glass bridge and cantilevered stairs.

The lower level is the real footprint of the house; this is where we meet the grass plateau of the dune where the house sits. Our "open pocket" doors unite the living and dining rooms to the sea air when needed, and the spatial plan of living room, dining room, and kitchen brings these entities together as a unified effort. At the other side of the lower space is the private area of a master bedroom, bath, office, and dressing rooms. The master bath telescopes to a smaller pavilion, where a three-sided, twenty-two-foot-tall mirrored vanity lives.

The kitchen is unique because it has no upper cabinets. All storage is addressed in automated drawers and a hidden wall pantry. The island stone top is a single piece of Blue Bahia imported from Brazil. The backsplash above the Corian counter is a six-foot piece of back-painted low-iron glass, which reflects light youthfully as the sun moves about outside. The exhaust hood for the stove is three pieces of glass that rises up out of the island on request and then disappears when no longer needed, much like the architect. Looking back up from the beach to the house and grounds, what was once two small cottages that introduced themselves to you on arrival is now a full collection of shapes and architectural gestures toward Martha's Vineyard traditional building types.

ust staggering: stacked and shifted pavilions each
ıke on their own heroic identity.
ı the foreground, three linked structures that
ouse the cars and generator set the scene
ɔr what awaits, as one approaches the house
nd the constant horizon of the sea.

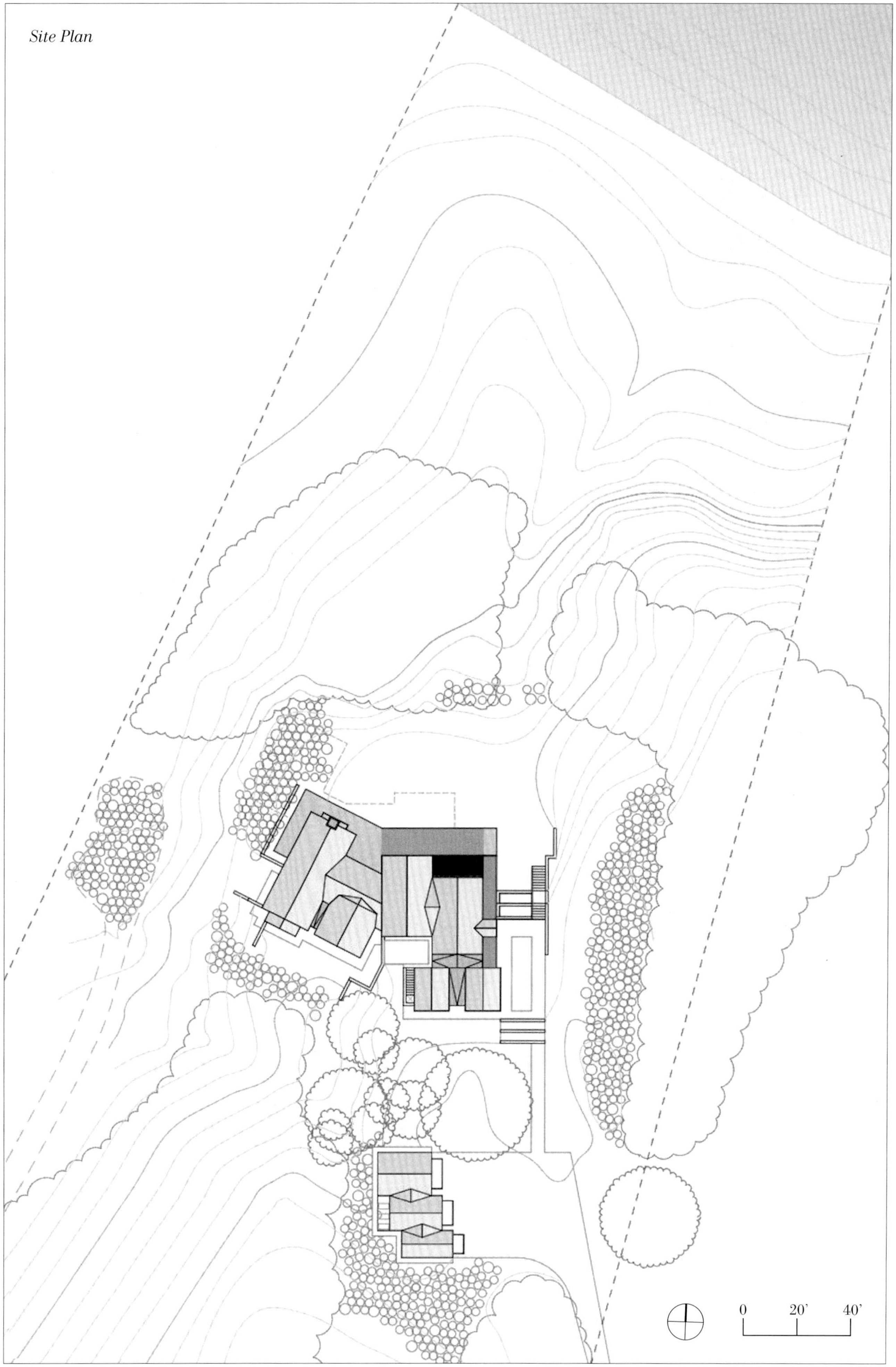

Upper Floor Plan

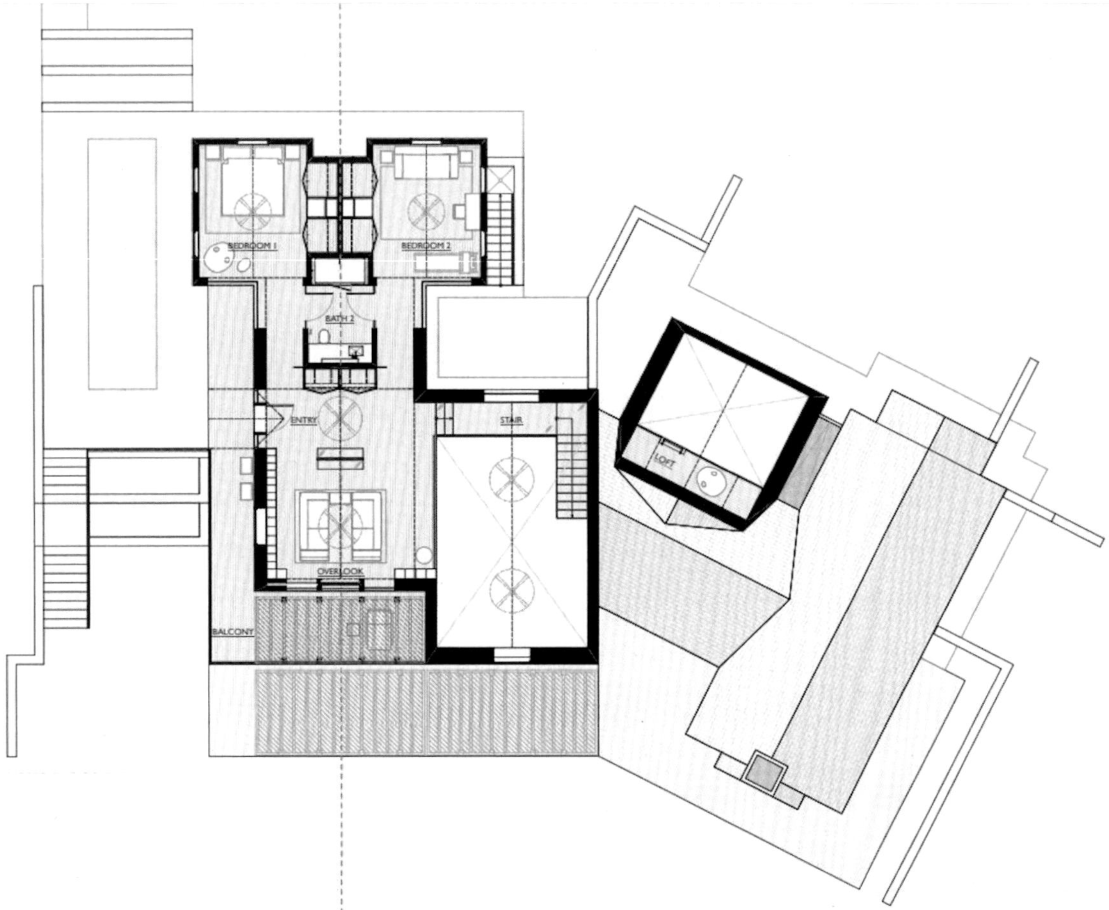

Lower Floor Plan

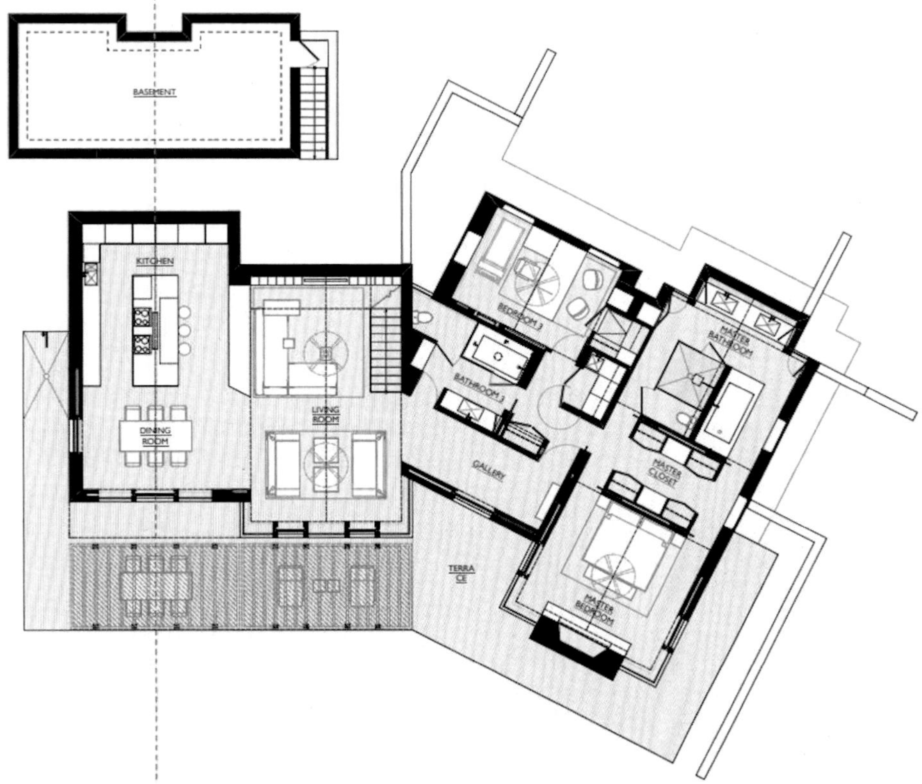

The design of the approach was intentionally modest. Unassuming structures removes the idea of the typical trophy beach house. Here, the buildings intersect with each other and sit on the lap of Martha's Vineyard sea grasses and bleached white oyster shells.

Tight, machine-like detailing, and the natural bleaching of the cedar shingles under the Massachusetts island sun, allows the different forms to both play about and also interlock with each other.

The little gable appears to float above the sea and sand.

A glass stair and bridge spans across a comfortable reading area. A glass wall to the entrance, library, and guest rooms invites the light to those areas.

At the time of this design, Hugh Jacobsen was having difficulty with many things in his life. Simon Jacobsen's feelings of sadness and the nostalgia for Hugh's earlier works led him to design this telescoping master bathroom (opposite) as an homage to him and his Buckwalter Telescope House of 1982. The owner agreed to the plan.

SPY HOUSE

Alexandria, Virginia

Occupying two conjoined apartments that hold two prominent corner spaces in a concrete 1970s Brutalist-designed high-rise, the natural feeling of skepticism was lurking in me as I entered the lobby for the ride up in the elevator.

Apartments are not easy to design well, in part, because of the orbital locality of the neighbor's services and utilities and the politics of the building. As with anything that is worth doing and especially worth doing well, the first question is always how does the archtiect fix the most glaring problem and what is the right thing to do.

In this case, the space suffered from the previous owner's aesthetic misfortunes, but it had sweeping one-hundred-eighty-degree views of both Washington and Alexandria on the Potomac. The client and the architect both agreed that the elan of the place was reminiscent of the Tom Hanks movie *Charlie Wilson's War*.

The owners were not the firm's usual client; they were former, very senior intelligence officers (hence the project name), and because they were so familiar with the firm's past work, they were issued an interoffice code name: *Legacy*.

The initial design motivation was very simple: straighten out the spaces, unify as many rooms with a singular unifying thoroughfare, or *a Rue*, as the architict calls it, and make them an intuitive and fluid movement with cross axis interaction of light and art. This is right out of the Baroque plans of European architecture. Then, imagine your clients entertaining and living normally in a space that is designed to do several different things at once.

The space needed to accommodate fifty guests in different seating groups and required a kitchen that was accessible on two sides, and have a bar, hidden pantries, and closets—and a nook to feed the dog. In the living room is a hidden theater behind faux walls and a translucent resin bar that overlooks the southern approaches of the city. Next to these is a secret fold-out office that is fitting for even MI6.

With all of the firm's interiors, seating groups are defined by an island of carpet. This allows for a stronger visual discipline in the organization of the space, especially in the relationships between furniture and objects and their carefully considered distances to each other.

The long hall that unites each of the spaces is adorned at either end with full-height floor-to-ceiling frosted panels, so as to fill the hall with daylight from either side; at night, they glow like a distant city.

The space has Jacobsen X-tables and refractory Lucite back-tables. Any time the firm is met with a back-of-couch conundrum, they use the refractory tables to display the owner's books, objects, and Jacobsen signature lamps, which provide a vital, directed, dimmed glow that completes the anticipation and delivers on the promise.

Floor Plan

Jacobsen refrectory and X-tables are the key to success in a modular seating group. The refrectory tables block the uninteresting back of couches and enforce the space's compartmentalized mission; the X-tables set the rhythm of the concept.

FDR
LINDSEY DAVIS
NICHOLSON BAKER
TITAN
ANITA HUFFINGTON
HORSE SOLDIERS

The all-Corian kitchen, including cabinets and drawer fronts, is a first in a design of this kind. The backsplash is not stainless, but a frosted, low-iron mirror-backed surface that provides ghosted reflections and light.

SPRING TRAIL

Stowe, Vermont

The seven-gabled house in Stowe was designed for two families from the Boston area who required a ski getaway in the Green Mountains.

Six pavilions, each with its own use, were laid out all connected by a long unifying corridor. From here, the staggered rooms and functions spring off the central axis from this "street." Unifying the plan and giving some centrality to the main hall, a fitted leather bench with piping and buttons that would make Mies van der Rohe wink sits on center with the dining room. Drawers are located under it for storage of ski boots and shoes.

The house is fitted with two equal but different master bedrooms and then two additional bedrooms behind each, all with en suite baths.

A glass cupola and skylight sits above the dining room table, balancing the light during the day.

Deployed in the living room was the firm's iconic corner-less glass and fireplace. On either side of these are Jacobsen signature open-pocket sliding doors with German lift-and-slide hardware in near-invisible recessed tracks. The trick to these is to make them appear as if they are really a fixed piece of glass, but on close inspection, or when trying to flee, it is clear that they are actually a door. This is accomplished by building out the jambs on the interior so the sides of the door can't be seen and no hardware is visible. Eggcrate bookcases adorn the opposite wall and rise to ten feet, framing the entrance and front door.

Floor Plan

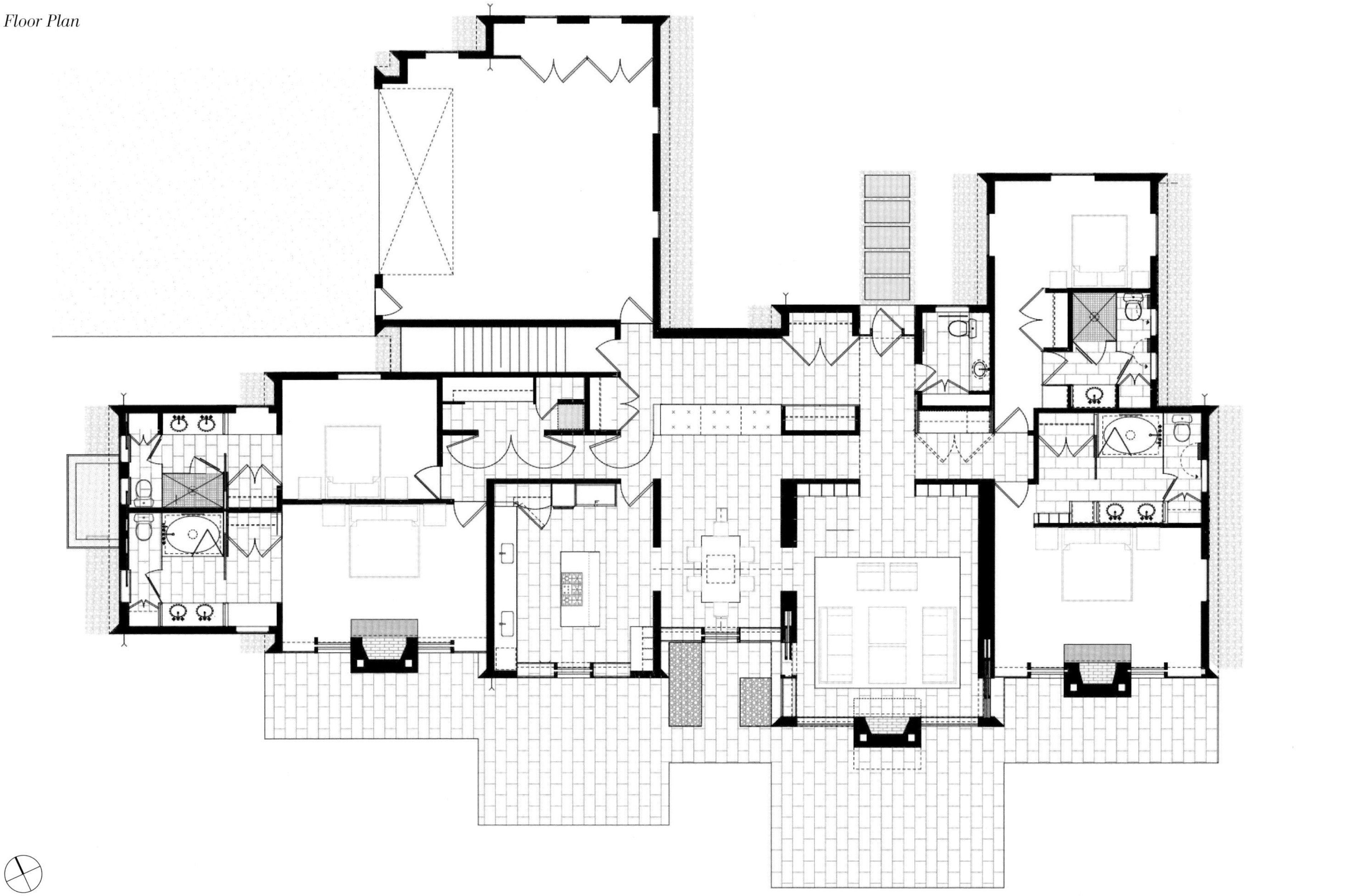

The madness is very much intentional: a rather traditional approach of the entrance is in stark contrast to the rear of the house. As the house meets the road and the neighbors, it is one thing, but as you move to the back, the house lets her hair down to reveal her real personality.

HARBOR HILL

Nantucket, Massachusetts

On the part of Nantucket Island that is known as Shimmo sits a house that is almost a village unto itself.

Traditional Nantucket architecture is often made up of smaller buildings, added and joined together as fortunes grow or as needed for an expanding family. It is only in town that the buildings begin to take on a mono-block shape due to the smaller land they occupy.

Two and a half miles outside of the town is Harbor Hill. The twenty-three-thousand-square-foot collection of New England building forms was built for a young American businessman who had sought out the firm originally for a different project, one in the Hamptons. The owner's requirements for the new house were vast and exciting, but the design problem of keeping such a structure "smallish" in such a bucolic and impossibly charming locale was the challenge.

On the site was a Queen Anne Revival house that had surely seen better days. The new owner aptly named it Mildew Manor and although the Jacobsens do not like removing old houses, reluctantly, plans were readied for its demise and disappearance from the five-acre lot.

The owner's program called for an eleven-bedroom house, kitchen, butler's pantry, dining room, formal living room, a large multiuse gathering space off the kitchen called the Friends' Room, a *hangar de rempotage*, three bars, male and female bathrooms for entertaining, gymnasia, staff quarters, two bedrooms for pilots, a theater, and game room, as well as sweeping views and outdoor seating areas overlooking Nantucket Harbor and town.

The proposition was to ensure that the size of the house could not be detected initially by the visitor or as you come up the bleached-oyster shell drive. The gate and fence are intentionally low-key. As you ascend the driveway, the first glimpse of house is of the exterior form of the master bedroom: a smallish, minimally detailed shingled pavilion with white trim and forty-five-degree roof plane of white cedar shingles. As you continue on, another smaller pavilion of similar size reveals itself, and then the main entrance unfolds like a newspaper.

In order to emphasize the singular, strong building forms, glass links were used to connect the pavilions. The use of glass links is paramount to the design because the rules on the island do not permit secondary buildings, therefore, connecting them all together in glass beat that part of the code and allowed the firm to achieve the "fishing village of one's own" that the site so badly needed.

Some of the largest pieces of glass available (in this case, fourteen feet by fourteen feet) were employed at different intersections; doors and windows, all designed by the firm, were adorned with the exaggerated Nantucket plank frame window that Nantucket architecture is known for.

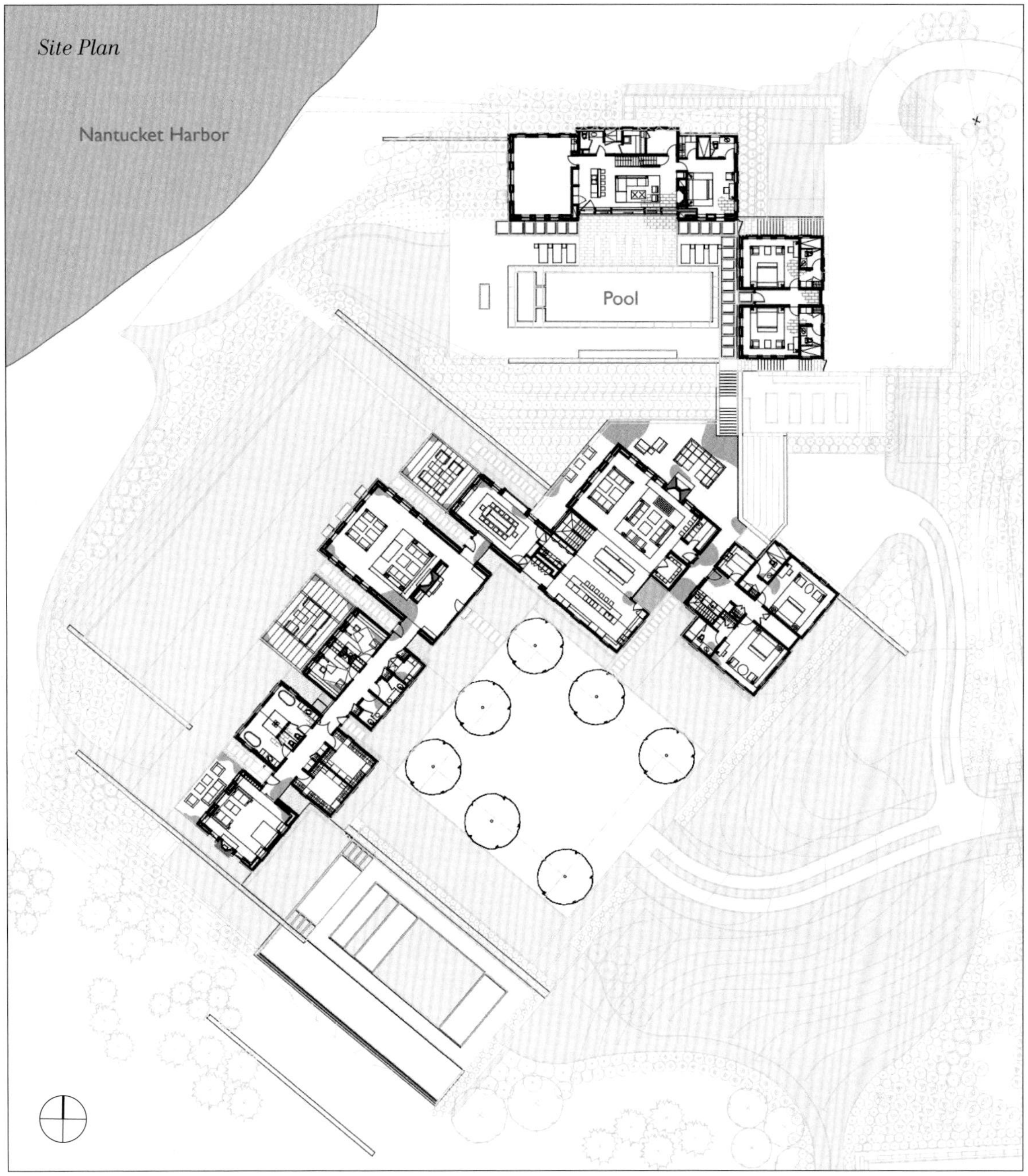
Site Plan
Nantucket Harbor
Pool

The intentionally sparse detailing and the refined lines underline the pristine nature of the house in its simplest form. Here, gutters have been removed and windows have been inset to create deep shadows as the sun moves.

Linking the pavilions together in glass allows for each building to show itself more heroically and express its own individual quality.
The glass links also allow for the views of the sea and fields from either side of the building, which helps erase the visual wall that so many houses accidentally create.

Main House - Front View

Main House - Harbor View

The unifying "street," an often long sunlit hall in Jacobsen buildings that organizes the spaces that come off it, establishes the order for the many spaces it serves.

The owner had a particular request concerning how the kitchen and casual spaces would be realized. The house has a formal dining room and butler's pantry, but it also includes, per the owner's desire, a casually combined space off the kitchen for light entertaining and lounging with friends. A fiber-optic-lit wine vault can be seen on the left, and a ten-foot-by-twelve-foot piece of glass allows for a view of the sea and white oyster-shell driveway.

A separate dining room seats twelve guests. Beyond it is the butler's pantry. A black "kerf" outlines the gables and walls and creates the illusion of floating walls and planes.

The second floor of the pool house has a gallery that looks down over the kitchen and juice bar. This space links two bedrooms and their own baths. The pool house also includes bedrooms below as well as a gymnasium and staff quarters.

BRAY HOUSE
THE BELLE OF THE BALL

Kittery Point, Maine

"I am really twenty-five, but I look fifty because of Bray House."

—Simon Jacobsen

Bray House was built in 1663 (I have had to preface the project by saying "That is not the address, but the date…") by John Bray, who was a Loyalist to the Crown. The house was small by today's excessiveness but it had appointments that were impressive for an eighteen-hundred-square-foot house. She didn't have an architect; very few did in the colonies then, most of the good ones being designed from so-called pattern books. The building's exterior was so plain that the architect could not find even a reference to anything like it in the seventeenth-century examples researched, but the interior millworks, fireplaces and volumes were completely from the books. Despite her appearance, Bray is a serious building.

For such a significant historical structure, Jacobsen was surprised and perplexed as to why it wasn't protected or on the historic register. The historic American Buildings Survey (HABS) had some information on it and in the 1940s *LIFE* magazine wrote about it with matronly photos of doilies and whale harpoons in every shot. These were used as a reference for what hard features stayed, which was basically everything.

Many of the townsfolk believed Bray House was actually this series of long, interconnected buildings—structures dating from 1888, 1919, 1930, and then 1945. The additions during the Great Depression were of the most concern. By the end of the World War II, tiny Bray House resembled a train of unassociated buildings squashed together and completely dominating the old house. When word got out that there were to be serious changes to the house, a town meeting was called where the architect presented the scheme to a group of one-hundred-fifty people who had very different ideas than his. Because the design was done by the book and followed the Secretary of the Interiors' guidelines for historical renovation, it was passed by the town council; but the architect still had to make it safely to his car in the parking lot; not everyone was thrilled by his presence...or cologne.

Old Bray had a serious problem. Its main supports were on two small ancient posts on opposite corners; what remained was supported on the corner of another building, which was not able to support even itself. The structure was a fascinating but primitive balloon frame, which made the problem worse, as it was just this tall bendy thing blowing in the wind and held together with wooden pegs and dovetails. It also leaned rather alarmingly seaward. Every interior door and window had a slanted head, and the first floor had a delightful vertical six-foot wave in it, as if it were mimicking Scandinavian bentwood.

The old girl had been given a great gift: new thoughtful owners with vision and a love for all things Maine. Upon the architect's initial visit, they asked, right off the bat, what he was going to do. He explained, at great risk to his future of being retained, that everything had to go except Bray herself; they would build a protective compound of white gables and glass around her to stabilize and protect, much like the arms of St. Peter's in Rome. In front of that will be a long pool and open-air summerhouse to finish off the composition "with commodity and delight," as Hugh would say.

Typically, they strangely didn't think he would take the job, and the architect was certain he wouldn't get the job.

However, despite the stabilization and renovation of the old house, the work started to manipulate the scale and proportion of the relationship between the old and new. Bray needed new everything on the outside, and because of the delicate nature of the ancient plaster interior, all electrical and HVAC work had to be done from the exterior while the siding was pulled off. A little bit of trickery was employed when the house was being straightened back into place; Jacobsen instructed the engineers to keep a five-degree tilt, so as to give it some romance and old wisdom.

In the design and resurrection of old buildings that are being given a second chance, quite often the designer is presented with a serious dilemma…or two hundred of them. The biggest one here was the question of how to treat the interior of the old house in a way that would take it by the hand to the twenty-first century and hopefully beyond. Great effort was made to repair and preserve the interior, but what then?

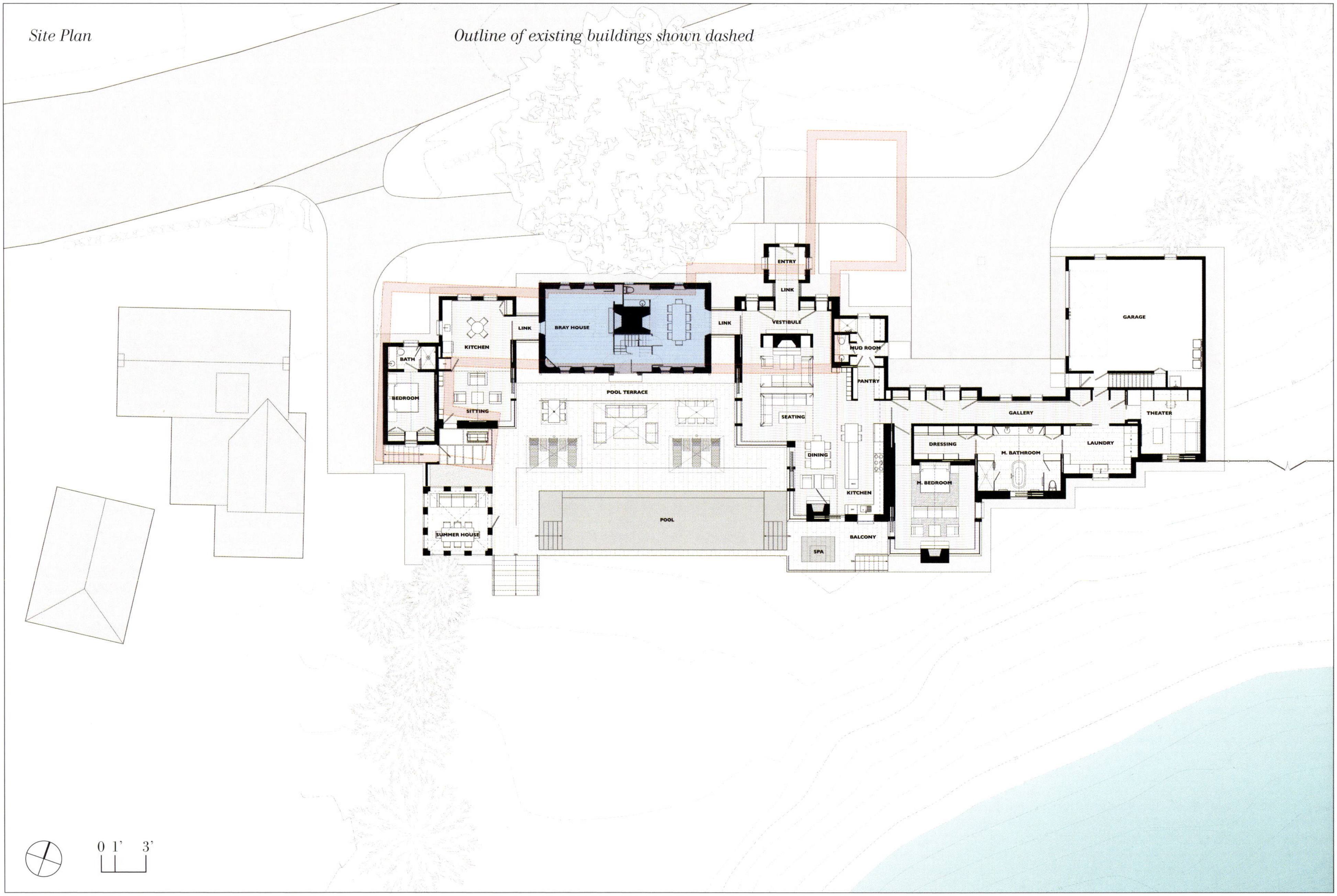

The red outline in the Bray House site plan shows the "situation" of the original buildings, which served only as a distraction to the more important old house, seen here in blue. It is not easy or comforting to remove older buildings, some as early as 1880, but their poor condition and planning made their surgical removal necessary to the survival of the main mission: Bray House.

The last thing the firm wanted to do was make yet another almost museum of yore and yawn. Therefore, the decision was made to *bronze it*. This meant painting all the interiors white, floors too, with a protective low VOC paint that would give the spaces a chic, fresh, and light-filled glow and prevent the damaging stripping of the delicate antiquities throughout.

Much ado was involved in the design of the seven thousand square feet of additions—a series of seven gabled pavilions that would stand off from, but protect, the revived manse. Glass links were designed to keep the house separated and to give a translucence and view from the road to the sea, a problem that had plagued her for one hundred years prior.

No addition could be taller than old Bray, and the width of any building had to be in units of thirds of the old house. This would ensure that Bray would keep its prominent place on the stage. Therefore, the ceiling heights of the new buildings were dropped to seven feet, but the interiors were volumetric and open to the ridges, so this was not detected. This reduced the overall roof height below Bray's. The next thing was to manipulate the siding. Bray had large seven-inch-to-the-weather white-wood clapboard. The additions would have a three-inch clapboard to trick the eye further to suggest that the new buildings were smaller and less dominant.

The design of the house is really about the relationship of openings and planes. Where one wall ends, there is a void, and then a plane starts again. In these voids are doors and tall pieces of glass. All the doors and openings are full height, with the exception of the square or rectangle casement windows that anchor down the vernacular to the neighborhood and, as well, the rest of New England.

The roofs are silver metal standing seam with inboard heated gutters for those Maine cold snaps. Regular outboard gutters have been eliminated to emphasize the linearity of the design of the roof planes and shape. The chimneys have a black stripe painted on them as a nod to John Bray himself. Houses loyal to the King in Massachusetts Bay, as it was called then, had a black stripe painted on the chimneys to alert other loyalists of their occupancy as well as to avoid possible bombardment by the British Navy.

South Elevation

Outline of existing buildings shown dashed

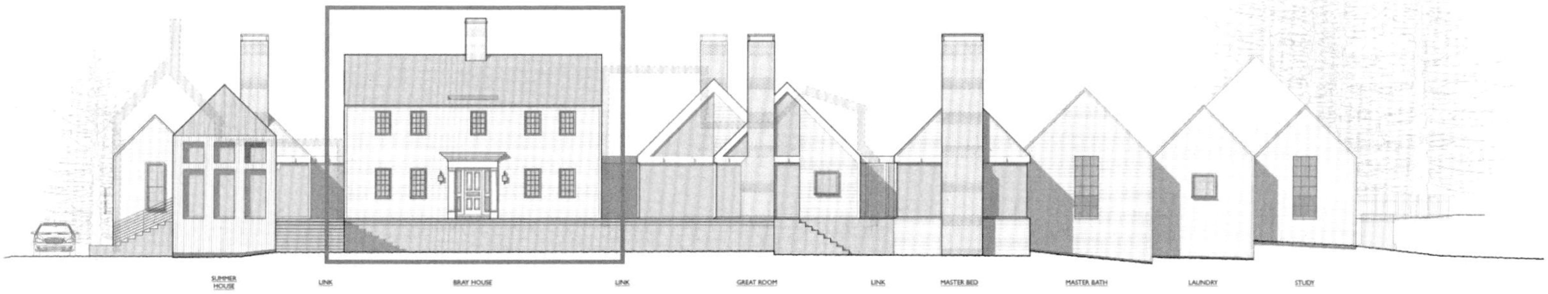

North Elevation

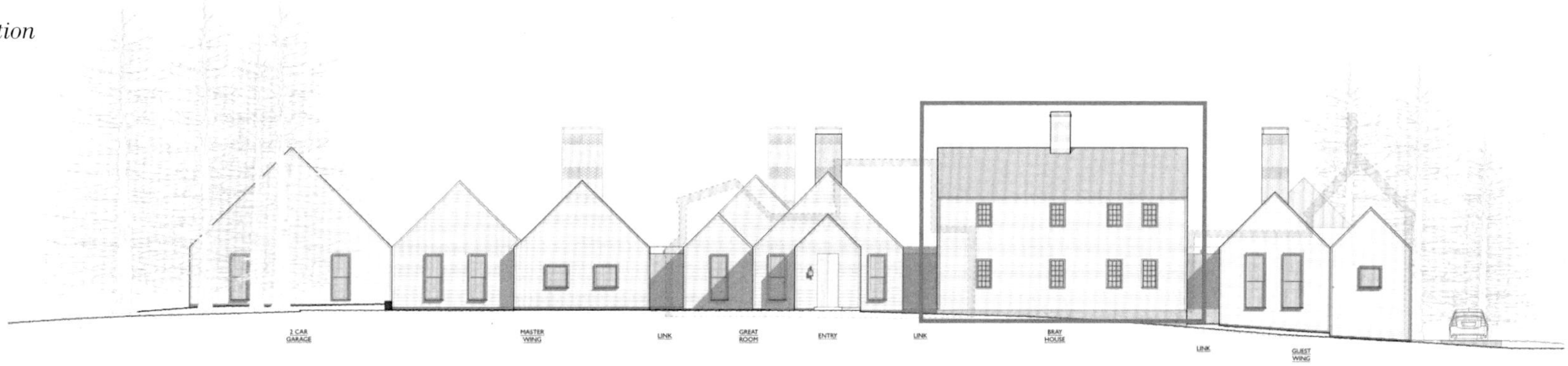

0 1' 3'

This is probably one of the more aggressive designs of a historic renovation and addition by the firm, however, it is not at all insensitive. Here we see the ultimate intent of the old house, already rather small: that it not be dwarfed by the new additions. The manipulation of scale and offset massing creates the illusion that the old house, long swallowed up by earlier additions, is once again the talent on the set.

The order and rhythm of early New England Greek Revival structures is one of the most poetic collection of forms. Often arranged piece by piece out of necessity rather than artistic or societal consideration, the little gabled pavilions throughout Maine turn and twist as needed. Here, off-set glass links separate the masses and allow for a translucent viewport to the sea. Borrowed from the Lady Pepperrell House and the First Congregational Church of Kittery Point just down the road are the distinctive windows and plank frame design—windows stand proud in the facade.

Small, ten-foot-wide pavilions are stepped back, allowing for shadows that emphasize depth and prevent the appearance of flatness. The wood siding on the new additions is small by half, allowing for a play of scale. A cleanly detailed metal standing-seam roof in concert with the small buildings reminds one that the design is in discourse with an earlier time in America.

Left and next spread
A visiting architect once referred to the pool house as a folly, and, keeping in mind the house's late seventeenth-century roots, it was intended as exactly that—and it was taken right from Sir Banister Fletcher's Global History of Architecture. *The rhythm and form changes to show that this is something different and that one may retire and repair here. The siding is now vertical, the roof is a pyramid, and, like a true folly, the scale is tricking you and slightly smirking.*

"I see no reason that if you live in an old house it has to be a testament to the ages; however, it has to reflect its origin, its original intent, character, and discipline. After that, your responsibility as the architect is to ensure its safety in the future with a bold but thoughtful design."
—Simon Jacobsen

CREMANT DU ROI
VEUVE AMIOT

ROCKPORT HOUSE

Rockport, Maine

"The site is impossible, the budget is absurd, but the clients are divine. We will make it work."

—Hugh Newell Jacobsen, lunch meeting at The Prime Rib, Washington, D. C.

This unique single-family house was a departure from the norms for both the architects and the clients. The owners reached out to the firm as an almost fluke because they thought the architects would never take something like this (wrong); and they found themselves designing a building that was crunched by the schedule and the laws of physics. The house is sited on a hill that has a forty-five-degree slope down to the rocky Maine coast and seaport of Rockport, and the design challenge was to not make the house primarily all basement as it stood proud like a sentry.

The clients are a couple who are the town's real estate agent and veterinarian. The site was rather small, so a two-story plan was needed to accommodate the four-bedroom layout. When faced with this kind of topography, how does one avoid the suburban walk-out scenario? The answer was to bring both decks and sunscreens down to the grade simultaneously while maintaining the simplicity and vertical linearity of the columns, door openings, and glass planes. Because the earth falls away so fast, two levels of balconies were required, as well. It is not often in the composition between landscape and house where both the roof pitch and land are forty-five degrees and match. This is one reason why the all-white structure sits so naturally on this brutal, rocky site.

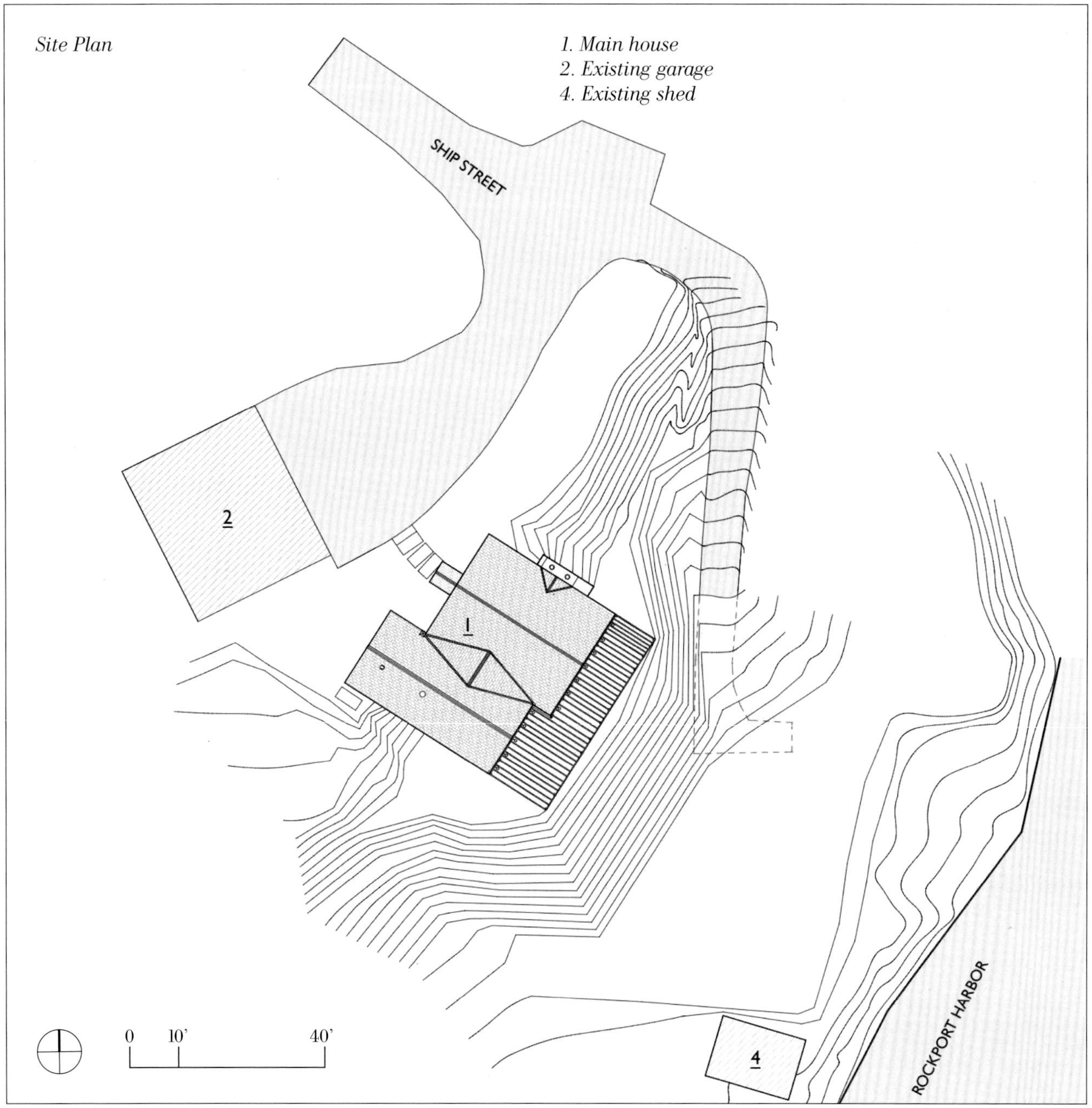
Site Plan
1. Main house
2. Existing garage
4. Existing shed
SHIP STREET
2
1
4
ROCKPORT HARBOR
0
10'
40'

Entry level floor plan

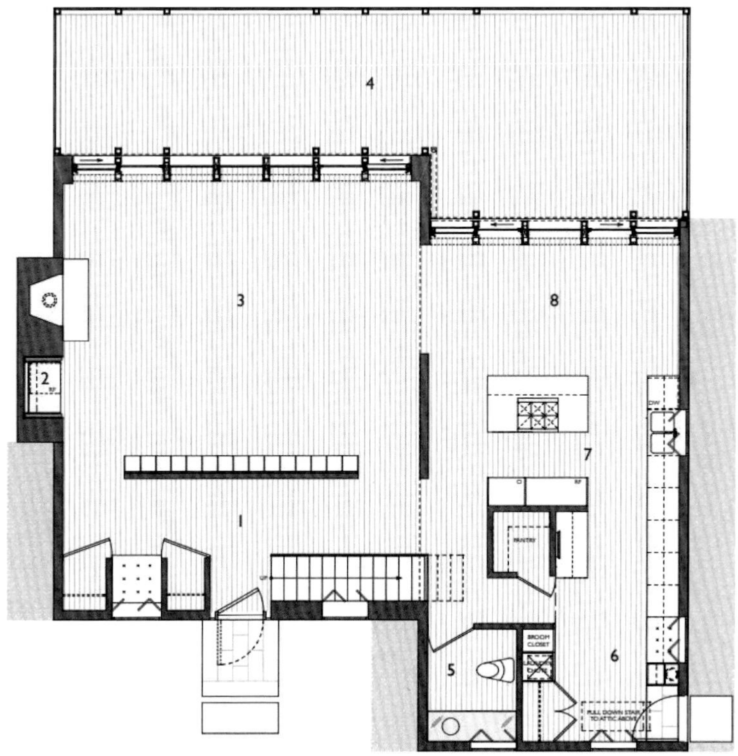

Lower level floor plan

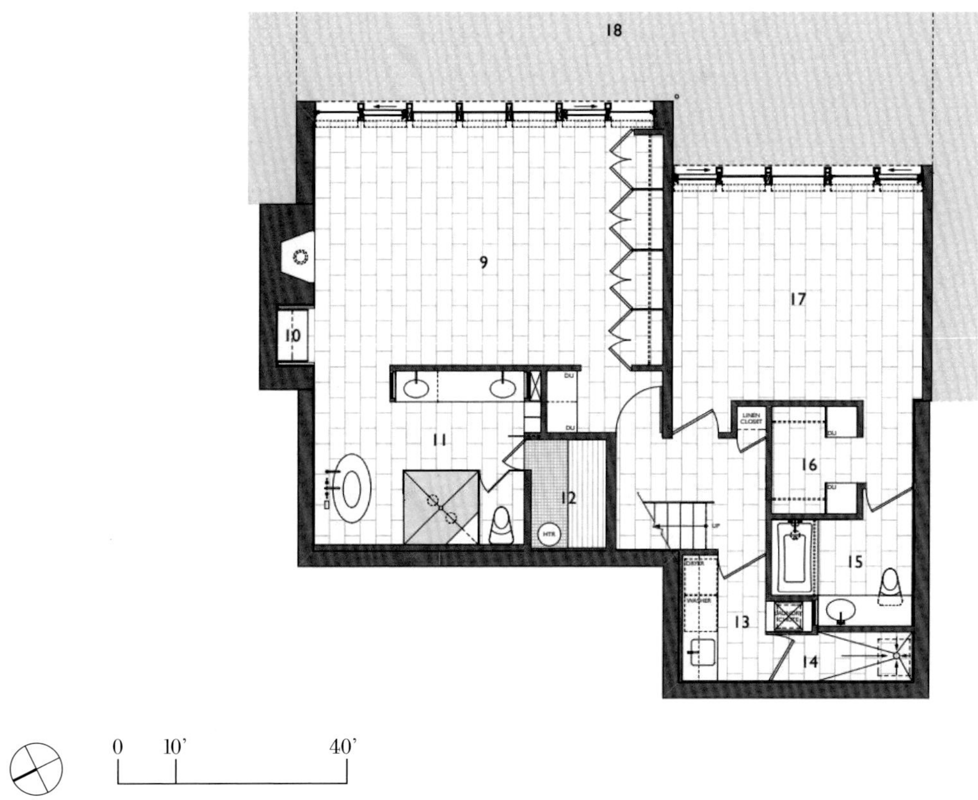

The floor plan reflects a very traditional Maine living style; a kind of skewed Baroque two-pile plan. In this unique house, the public spaces are on the top level and the private spaces are below.

The black stripe is an age-old Jacobsen detail; it is a continuous eave vent that allows air into the attic and roof. It also has an insect screen behind it to prevent passing winged ones from gaining unwelcome entry.

The collision of the roof forms, tall planes, and voids allows for a kind of dance that takes place within Rockport House. Pitched gabled ceilings rest comfortably on the interior of the butterfly wall, a void is created, and the wall next to it becomes a bookshelf.

Ballistic-glass windows were designed to face the sometimes harsh North Atlantic exposure. Beyond these is a steel-reinforced sunscreen that gives a shadow dance across the deck and furniture.

The beauty of this ocean view results, in part, from its being broken up by the land, which prevents any monotony that may arise from the constant horizon of the sea. In such matters, it is always a comparison of one thing to the other. The deck is an eco-friendly product made from recycled Clorox bottles.

Do not build on the hill, build of the hill, said Frank Lloyd Wright—an admonition embraced here. Not doing so ruins the natural beauty of the landscape.

WINDSOR

Vero Beach, Florida

The Windsor Code, as it is known, will give pause to any architect who builds there. Written by the development's owner and Andres Duany and Elizabeth Plater-Zyberk, the code is not at all Jacobsen-friendly, but the firm managed to build five houses there and much of them the architects consider their best work.

The carefully planned, polo-centric seaside village borrows its aesthetic from the early Latin Caribbean building forms and details, all mostly within protective walled compounds.

The owner, a German gentleman who simply stated he was a farmer, required a substantial house that would encompass half a block for his visiting adult children and grandchildren. It includes a master bedroom on the ground floor and two additional apartments with two bedrooms each overlooking the pool and palms of the enclosed garden.

A sunscreen mitigates the hot Florida southeastern sun and casts dramatic shadows of opposing angles. The use of white ground coral in poured concrete in one-by-two-foot sizes establishes the linearity of the walks and takes your eye in the direction intended. The black-bottom pool aligns itself with an open-air summerhouse where one can repair from the hot sun for a bit. Opposite the pool and summerhouse is a sculpture by Lady Pixie Shaw, a friend of the owners and also of Windsor.

The buildings themselves are of stucco with silver standing-seam roofs that evoke earlier simple Florida agricultural forms. One of the challenges of this kind of layout is where to put the air conditioner condensers. Open exterior attics were designed where the architects could slide the units in on the roof and not have them on the ground or be seen or heard.

All of the doors and windows were custom designed. The use of Jacobsen "open pocket" doors allow for a virtually trackless and hidden lift-slide hardware.

First-Floor Plan

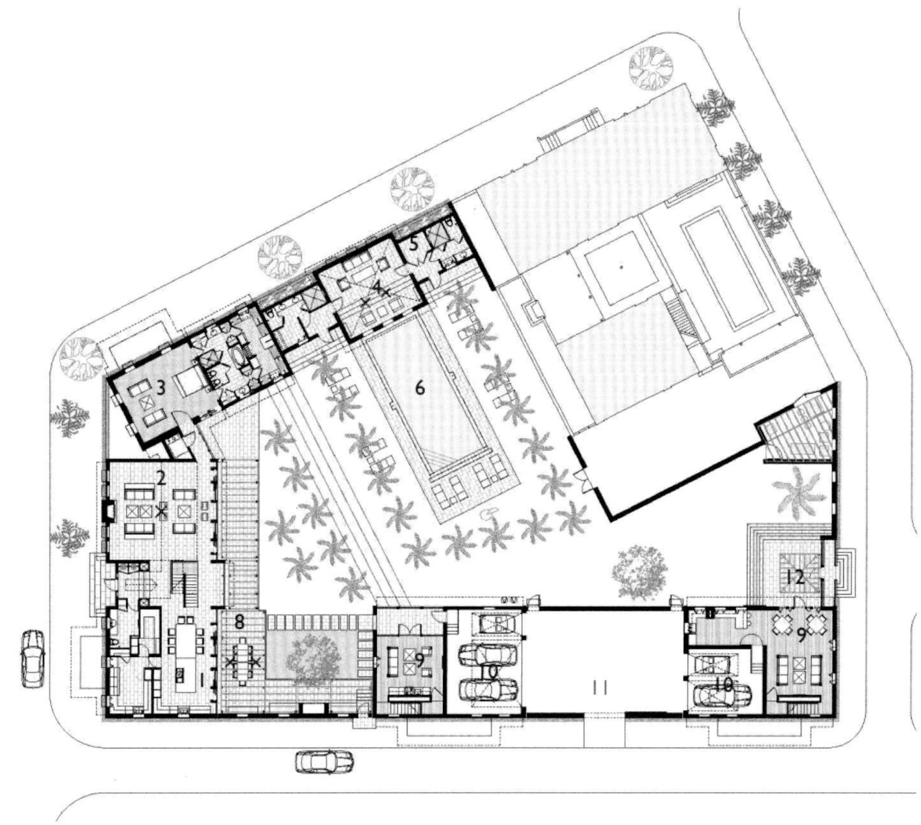

Second-Floor plan

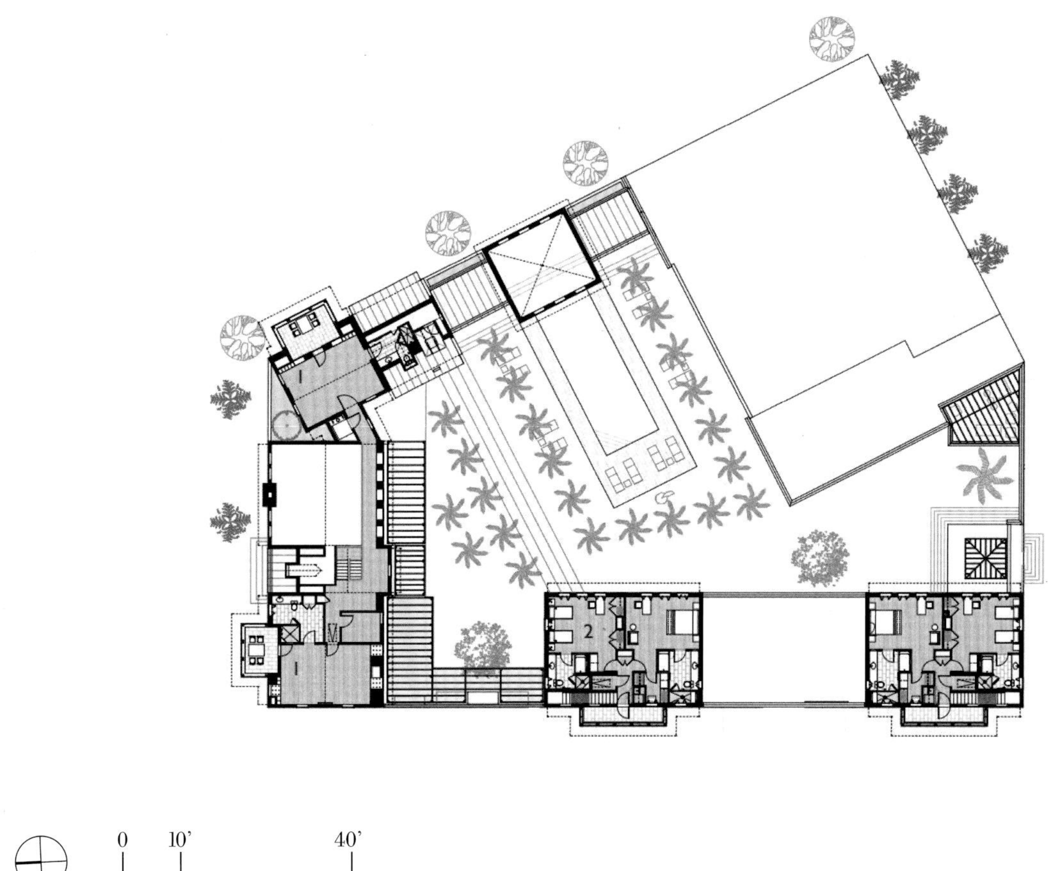

A combination of the Windsor Code and the owner's wish for a Spanish Colonial–style walled hacienda centralizes the gathering point around the stepped gardens and pool.

ABERCROMBIE
STOP

ACKNOWLEDGMENTS

First and foremost, for Ruth, who brings me back to earth when the challenges of life can meet a piercing crescendo—she reminds me that "It's just a thing."

The firm is, and always will be, what is called a "critical practice," simply set forth by my father's intensity and drive: an artistic rhythmic frenzy, above all else, to solve problems that were biting at him, often two hundred at a time. How he ever managed to look up from his graph paper sketch pad and travels long enough to groom me into the profession of architecture and design is still very much a mystery to me today. My mother, as well, was also a driving force behind the unusual and even controversial movement to have me ultimately head up the Jacobsen firm. It should be noted, however, that they were not ever the type of parents of the New Age method of parenting whose encouragement was issued in singsong loving spoonsful at every encounter—quite the opposite. They were rigid in their guidance, and suspicious of the unfamiliar, if I swayed off course away from the profession. In a way, this was also a critical practice for them, too. I shall be ever grateful for their love and support, and also for what they instilled in me, especially the idea that what we are doing here "…is not a dress rehearsal."

A practice as intense as this one has its set of members who contribute and are as important to the design of any given project as its architect. They are professionals who are so attuned to the work and the unusual detailing, that the language of the firm becomes second nature to them, as well. Their consistency and discipline contribute to the success and culture of the designs.

My gratitude goes out to architect Richard Cho. Ever cool and levelheaded, dedicated to the practice for the past twenty-five years, his talent is well represented in almost all the projects in this book. His ability in planning and problem-solving is unmatched.

Jon Althiemer, our "constant agent of change," came to us fifteen years ago as an office assistant. A few months after joining, he informed me that he had passed the bar exam a few months earlier. Almost immediately, he became our new business manager and in-house legal counsel. Today, he is an expert in the sometimes sticky contract negotiations of the company—a steady guiding hand in an occasionally dark and choppy sea.

About half of the beautiful images in this book are the work of our late friend, the legendary photographer Robert C. Lautman (recipient of the AIA Gold Medal for Architectural Photography). He is much missed. Bob and Hugh were best friends until the end, and he was surely one of the people who helped put Jacobsen Architecture in the world view.

As a young apprentice architect just out of school, I watched closely some of the highly talented senior architects then working, such as Paul Roddick and Luther Weber, who had both mastered the method of navigating complex buildings and complex clients while balancing the challenges presented in their own lives, all without ever missing a step.

Architect Ernie Schichler, who retired toward the completion of Harbor Hill, was a presence of professionalism and constant calm. Many of his solutions, and "the thing that just works," are still used today, and can be seen in every project in this volume. He helped set a standard of design and methods, saying to Hugh and me on several occasions, "That is not what we do." And he was right.

Architect Heidi Leinbach, who we affectionately called the Hammer, executed many unique and beautiful details. Evidence of this can be seen here in Honeymoon Cottage, Harbor Hill, Spy House, and Bray House, to name only four. She got her nom de guerre from her method of counseling contractors, who never dared sway away from the design in the slightest.

Paul Goldberger is a household name in news and architectural circles, where I thought my name would never cross his keyboard. He wrote the introduction to Hugh's last book, which made Goldberger even more of a hero in our office and house. I am very grateful and so honored that he has written the introduction here. When I spoke to him initially on the phone, I stood up. The second time I was to speak with him, I put on a tie.

But where would all this be without Rizzoli editor Douglas Curran? I reached out to him in 2019 BC (Before COVID) with the idea of a new book, fully expecting a very polite, "Thank you, but no." (I had two other appointments with publishers that day. When I called them to cancel, one editor interrupted me, and said, "Let me guess,

you went to Rizzoli first?") Throughout pandemic delays and the laws of physics that always get in the way, the process and the project has been a joy to work on, thanks to him and to the book's designer, Beatriz Cifuentes, who also worked for the legendary Massimo Vignelli—who designed Hugh's three other monographs.

There is a feeling of full circle here, but one very important person is missing: the Great Man.

INDEX

BIOGRAPHIES

Simon Jacobsen is a founding partner of the internationally acclaimed architectural firm Jacobsen Architecture, LLC, with his father, Hugh Newell Jacobsen, FAIA. He works throughout the United States, the Caribbean, Europe and Asia, and the primary focus of his work is custom residential, commercial, and institutional design, as well as interiors, furniture, and lighting design. Simon Jacobsen is a recipient of many prestigious awards in the field and has been honored by the American Institute of Architects, the Society of American Registered Architects, and *Architectural Digest*, where he is an inductee of the coveted AD100. Simon Jacobsen is married with two children and lives in Delaplane, Virginia.

Hugh Newell Jacobsen (1929–2021) was born in Grand Rapids, Michigan. He was trained as an architect at Yale University and studied under Louis Kahn. Afterwards, he worked for Philip Johnson and then opened his own office in 1959. In 1971, Mr. Jacobsen became a Fellow of the American Institute of Architects, and, in 1992, he was elected an Academician of the National Academy of Design. In 2009, with Simon Jacobsen, he cofounded the new firm Jacobsen Architecture, LLC. Widely acclaimed, he received more than one hundred twenty awards for his work, including six national honor awards from the American Institute of Architects and twenty awards for excellence in house design from *Architectural Record*.

CREDITS

Bird House
Napa, California
Staff Architect: Mark Johnson
Architectural Photography: Douglas Sterling; pp. 18–19 © Roger Davies / OTTO; and pp. 20–21, 34 by Simon Jacobsen

Smith Row
Georgetown, Washington, D. C.
Staff Architect: Richard Cho
Architectural Photography: Robert C. Lautman

Honeymoon Cottage
Kennett Square, Pennsylvania
Interior Design: Jacobsen Architecture
Staff Architect: Heidi Leinbach
Interior Coordinator: Lindsay Clark
Architectural Photography: Simon Jacobsen; and pp. 57, 62–63, 65 Genevieve Garruppo, Architectural Digest © Condé Nast

Chic Convenience
Georgetown, Washington D. C.
Staff Architect: Richard Cho
Architectural Photography: Robert C. Lautman

Calvert Street Apartment
Washington, D. C.
Interior Design: Jacobsen Architecture
Staff Architects: Richard Cho, Lynne Stokes
Architectural Photography: Anice Hoachlander

Beach House
Aquinnah, Massachusetts
Staff Architects: Richard Cho, Lynn Stokes
Architectural Photography: Simon Jacobsen

Spy House
Alexandria, Virginia
Staff Architects: Heidi Leinbach, Greg Thomas, AIA
Architectural Photography: Simon Jacobsen

Spring Trail
Stowe, Vermont
Interior Design: Jacobsen Architecture
Architectural Photography: Douglas Sterling

Harbor Hill
Nantucket, Massachusetts
Staff Architects: Heidi Leinbach, Ernest Schichler, Richard Cho.
Architectural Photography: Simon Jacobsen
Interior Coordinator: Lindsay Clark

Bray House, the Belle of the Ball
Kittery Point, Maine
Staff Architects: Mark Johnson, Heidi Leinbach, Richard Cho
Architectural Photography: Jonathan Reece

Rockport House
Rockport, Maine
Staff Architect: Richard Cho
Architectural Photography: Richard Mandelkorn

Windsor
Vero Beach, Florida
Staff Architect: Richard Cho
Architectural Photography: Simon Jacobsen